MW00738081

The World's Leading Real Estate Experts
Reveal the Secrets to Selling Your Home
for Top Dollar in Record Time!

Published by CelebrityPress™, Orlando, FL
A division of The Celebrity Branding Agency®

Celebrity Branding® is a registered trademark
Printed in the United States of America.

ISBN: 9780983947011
LCCN: 2011936942

This publication is designed to provide accurate and authoritative information with regard to the subject matter covered. It is sold with the understanding that the publisher is not engaged in rendering legal, accounting, or other professional advice. If legal advice or other expert assistance is required, the services of a competent professional should be sought. The opinions expressed by the authors in this book are not endorsed by CelebrityPress™ and are the sole responsibility of the author rendering the opinion.

Most CelebrityPress™ titles are available at special quantity discounts for bulk purchases for sales promotions, premiums, fundraising, and educational use. Special versions or book excerpts can also be created to fit specific needs.

For more information, please write:

CelebrityPress™,

520 N. Orlando Ave, #2
Winter Park, FL 32789
or call 1.877.261.4930

Visit us online at www.CelebrityPressPublishing.com

The World's Leading Real Estate Experts Reveal the Secrets to Selling Your Home for Top Dollar in Record Time!

Contents

CHAPTER 1

Why do up to 54.8% of Homes that go on the Market *Fail* to Sell?

By Jay Kinder

It's a shocking statistic isn't it? Unfortunately, it's been true in almost every year of my career; about half of the homes that go on the market fail to sell. Well, at least in their initial listing term. It is quite alarming if you are considering selling your home, and even worse if you really need to sell your home. How is it possible? I have an unusual insight as to why this is. In fact, for the first few years I was a real estate agent, I was unknowingly part of the problem.

Fourteen years ago, at the age of 19, I completed the 45 necessary "clock hours" needed to become a provisional real estate licensee in the state of Oklahoma. Looking back, I am not sure which is the most alarming, ... why I got into real estate, or, ... how easy it was.

Let me explain. My intentions were good when I decided to become a real estate agent, but it was not a career path. It was an abrupt change in my life that forced me into a "real job." I had a child on the way and was now married. In fact, you will find that most real estate agents were not on a career path that land-ed them in the field of real estate. The overwhelming majority chose real estate for the same reason that I did. It looked like it had some freedom and flexibility along with pretty good income potential. That or they lost their corporate job. Many real estate agents are part time. They do it on their own schedule helping friends and family with their purchases.

So what's the big deal? Well, the average real estate agent only sells five homes per year, invests an average of $232 per year into their business, and have only completed the mandatory training required by the state in order to give you advice on the largest investment you will ever make in your lifetime. An industry that is responsible for more than 17% of this country's GDP, and which controls the buying and selling of what represents 62% of the net worth of the average American is only required a few weeks (or months in some states) of training?

Well, if the American Dream is such an important part of our countries heritage, and plays such a significant role in our economy, wouldn't we want to make sure we have highly specialized professionals in these positions? ...especially since the amount earned on the average transaction is more than $11,435*. Could these part time, gun-slingin' agents be partly to blame for thousands of home owners who took on mortgages beyond their ability to pay in recent years? Who was advising these home buyers? Is it fair only to blame the mortgage industry? I can feel the red laser on my forehead. Tens of thousands, if not several hundred thousand agents out of the million plus in this field of work, are already plotting how to take me out. If not these agents, then who?

Let's take a look at what we are dealing with here. A real estate agent, which I have been for 14 years mind you, has to join a brokerage that is managed by a Broker. Surely there are procedures in place to manage the process which a buyer or seller goes through? Surely there are strict customer service regula-

*Estimate based on 6% commission and U.S. Average Sales Price.

tions in place that closely watch how the client is being advised? Surely the Broker plays an active role in the home-buying and home-selling experience to make sure certain measures are taken, proper advice is given, and continuous review of performance is exhibited…..or at least attempted? Nope, nope, and nope!

Starting to get the picture as to why more than half the homes that go on the market fail to sell? Well surely, major franchises, without naming names, have a much different approach than this. At least you would have better odds with one of them, right? …Wrong.

This is an industry-wide problem. The brokerages typically give away 70%-100% of the commissions to the agents, therefore the money that would be used to measure and or monitor the real estate transaction are not affordable. In fact, nearly every real estate agent out there is an "independent contractor," and by law, Brokers could not force them to even attend a meeting at their firm.

Let's look at another example. You have a home you want to sell, and of course you would like to sell it at the top of the market. The most the market will bear. You would probably agree that the price at which your home sells is elastic to all the variables involved in the home-selling process. Some of the variables are not within your control, such as interest rates, competition, market trends, availability of financing, and incentives offered by competing homes. We call these the "outside threats." They must be carefully noted and the advice given should take them into consideration on how you position your home to sell in the market. Make sense?

Then there are other variables; variables that ARE within your control or the control of your real estate agent such as condition, price, upgrades, professional marketing, exposure to the marketplace, negotiation, cooperation with other agents, and execution across all these variables. If these variables are managed properly you will attract a higher offer, and if managed poorly, you will likely attract a much lower offer, that is if you attract an offer at all. Remember your odds, nearly 50/50.

I personally believe that there is a much better way to manage this process. It doesn't have to cost you more money to hire a team of specialists that can manage the entire process whereby you get a predictable result. There are three distinct variables you should look for in hiring an agent to sell your home or assist you in the process of making an investment in real estate.

They are as follows:

1. **Specialized Knowledge**

   This is more complex than just looking for how many letters an agent has behind their name, although that can be a good indicator that they care enough about their clients to continuously strive to gain more knowledge.

2. **Experience**

   Without question, I would hire an agent with a high level of success before ever hiring an agent that only sells a handful of homes per year. Everyone knows someone in real estate, it's your responsibility to make sure you hire a competent professional, and not just a friendly neighbor who holds a license.

3. **Proven, Repeatable Process**

   This could prove to be more of a challenge, which has become the purpose for my life. 'Winging it' is not a proven, repeatable process and if you only succeed half of the time then you certainly don't have a proven, repeatable, process that manages the consumer experience.

Look at it this way. If you were to hire a surgeon for a life-threatening surgery you would want to know that he or she was the foremost expert on the type of surgery you need, and you would also require that he had been successful with this exact surgery many times. You would also want to know that there was a specific process that he and his or her team would follow to ensure that success was achieved. Am I right? Thought so.

Having sold thousands of homes representing several hundred million dollars worth of real estate as a real estate agent, I can tell you that there is only one organization that is significantly changing the industry and that is the National Association of Expert Advisors: www.NAEA.com .

The prudent thing to do as a potential home buyer or seller is to seek out an Expert Advisor that is a part of this organization. They are truly the Expert Advisors in the real estate industry and hold themselves to a higher level of professionalism and expertise.

There truly is a difference between a real estate agent and an Expert Advisor.

About Jay

Jay Kinder is a business phenom – going from small town kid to master business growth strategist recognized throughout the real estate industry.

Nobody in the tiny town of Walters, Oklahoma, population 2,142, would have voted this notably ornery and average student most likely to become a millionaire, but that didn't stop him from building an impressive real estate brand, positioning him as one of the top 10 Coldwell Banker Agents Worldwide, Small Business Administration Young Entrepreneur of the Year, Realtor Magazine's 30 under 30, Wall Street Journal's top 25 agents worldwide, and a laundry list of high achievement awards all by the age of 30 years old. By the time Jay was 25 years old, he had become a local celebrity and brilliant strategist.

By the time he was 28 years old, his passion for real estate expanded as he and his business partner Michael Reese, a top agent that got into real estate after seeing Jay's incredible business success, decided to open the doors to their own successful businesses. They began recreating their own success by helping agents like themselves master massive growth and celebrity stardom in their own real estate markets.

This new business, Kinder Reese Real Estate Partners has been credited with helping thousands of real estate agents strategically growth their businesses with their proven and market-tested ideas. Jay and Mike now share a passion for growth-minded individuals who have a burning desire to add value to people's lives – while enjoying a higher quality of life.

CHAPTER 2

Realtor's Expertise and Experience define Customer Satisfaction

By Michael Reese

Why do so many homes that go on the market fail to sell? Have you ever thought about why some homeowners sell their home in 6 days for full price, while other homes seem to sit on the market like a potted plant? As a professional real estate agent, I have advised thousands of homeowners on selling their home. I have been recognized by the Wall Street Journal as one of the most successful agents in the country. This has given me a rare opportunity to train real estate agents all over the country – by taking an in-depth look at their business.

I understand what works, why some fail and others succeed almost effortlessly. My biggest take-away from all I have learned from these experiences is that all agents are not the same. The consumer has no idea what they will get in one part of the country, across town, or even in the same city with the same brokerage. Homeowners gamble everyday, with hope as the only strategy to getting their home sold.

During my observations of looking into office after office, business after business, and agent after agent, I did find one common theme or belief, if you will, among the top producers. Top producers were not a one-man army, they weren't unhappy with the market, and they weren't even shocked that they were growing while others continued to fail. They were what I call experts, but being an expert was just one part of the puzzle. They had the knowledge and could synthesize and communicate their knowledge effectively. They were what I refer to as *expert advisors*; the homeowner failed or succeeded based on their advice.

These Expert Advisors always put their clients interests above their own. They all educated their clients to a point where their clients knew what, how, why and everything in-between. The defining gap was clear the agents who had the desire to be the best, were all relentless seekers of knowledge. How these agents connected the dots initially was with passion and sure tenacity. I knew through this experience that success was in fact duplicatable for both the agent and the homeowner.

Initially, I got into the training business because I hated seeing agents struggle for decades trying to make it in this business. You see, there is a dirty little secret that most homeowners don't even realize. That secret is hidden behind nice clothes, business cards, and fast talk. That secret is that the traditional agent is fast-dying a rapid death. The reason can usually be traced back to the very reason they got into this business in the first place. Most agents did not leave successful marketing jobs or have any past business experience that would lend itself to success in real estate.

Most agents found their way into this career we call real estate as a default to a life crisis. The majority sell a handful of homes every year, and most importantly, work when they want to work. This is fine by me, and I feel very privileged to know my competition is more motivated by flexibility in work schedule than marketing.

How else would a 25-year-old kid become the number one agent in the fastest growing city in America? I became a relentless student of business, marketing, and then real estate. I did not have the most past clients, money, or experience. However I did have the absolute best training, from both my previous employer, and an amazing mentor. My mentor showed me the importance of investing in my own education. As my knowledge grew over 10 years, I started looking at the problem differently.

Witnessing so many agents fail made me become aware of the true victims. I started seeing families left in the wake of these agents shattered careers – families who had to sell, retirees who need their equity, and growing families who needed more home, all were saddened by the results of their agent. I realized then that I could either sit back and watch or I could do something about it. After discussing, and researching for almost an entire year, my business partner Jay Kinder and I aligned our core values and core competencies and set out to change a 100-year-old industry.

Now, as co-founder of the National Association of Expert Advisors, my life's purpose has become being a consumer advocate for homeowners. With research showing that both buying and selling a home being ranked as one of the most stressful times in one's life, we have made it our purpose to help consumers properly evaluate and hire the right person.

I truly believe if you hire the right agent who is properly trained, with real world experience, and has a proven track record, you can prevent most frustrations before you start by getting the correct advice. Advice that could mean, based on your goals, that it's not a good time to sell or buy. Advice from a true, trusted, Expert Advisor who puts your interest above their own.

The NAEA (National Association of Expert Advisors) provides agents who understand the cause of most of these frustrations a place to advance their knowledge and skills. It provides homeowners nationally with a consistency unmatched in consumer experience.

One of the most prestigious designations an agent can hold is a

Certified Home Selling Advisor designation.

Selling a home is definitely not an event, it is a process. As homeowners, we have the most control over this process by managing a few, but very important, events. If you look at this entire process in the form of a timeline, the most important event that is done wrong is also considered the biggest mistake of the homeowner. That is, <u>hiring the wrong real estate agent for the job of selling your home.</u>

If you have never heard of the Pareto principal, it states that, for many events, roughly 80% of the effects come from 20% of the causes. You see when you hire an agent that is not qualified to sell your home, you run the risk of making a wrong decision on the causes that affect if a home sells or sits on the market.

Price, Condition, and Marketing are just a few things that affect if a home sells or fails to sell. What I know to be true is there is no fixed price for selling a home, homes sell in a range. The range that all home's sell for is elastic to the condition of the property –which usually will either increase or decrease demand. What I have found is that it is a lot easier to negotiate an offer to full price, the higher the offer is made to the listing price. Since every homeowner would love to have a full-price offer, it is fair to say that "you want to have the highest possible offer, because the lower the offer the less likely you would come to an acceptable agreement."

As a Certified Home Selling Advisor I understand the importance of doing a thorough analysis up front to make sure my advice is in alignment with my client's goals. In the medical field, diagnosis before prognosis is considered malpractice. The traditional agent might not know or even care to ask the right question in order to give you the best advice. As an agent who carries the designation of CHSA, we are trained and certified in advising our clients based on the answers to very important questions that we must know, in order to give the right advice. Individually we all study and advance our expertise by passing an advanced exam in order to qualify to use the Expert Advisor Home Selling System.

The Expert Advisor Home Selling System takes into consideration several facts about the home selling process. One of the most important facts is that there are things that are in an agent's control, but most of those are affected by things out their control. Things that are out of control for a CHSA are the reason for selling, time frame, and the homeowner's financial goals –just to name a few. A CHSA is trained in the beginning to have the hard conversations up front; these conversations would be forbidden by a traditional agent because they could cause a homeowner not to sell or, even worse, choose another agent.

The Expert Advisor Home Selling System is designed to remove the elements that position a home to depreciate in the perception of value. It's objective is clear, proven and repeatable – deliberately removing things from the process that allow buyers to reach in your pocket after you have an accepted offer. Preventing them to use time-tested and foolishly-accepted practices to negotiate sometimes saves up to thousands more in the sale.

Equity is like energy in a negotiation, it's never lost, it simply changes hands during a real estate transaction. The Expert Advisor Home Selling System understands and obeys the Laws that govern these eighty-plus variables. It allows a homeowner to proactively manage these events throughout the process, allowing them to sell their home at the top of the market as opposed to the bottom of the market – by attracting the highest possible offer.

As the face of real estate continues to change, our goal was accomplished. We successfully built a system that allowed clients to have the best consumer experience; an experience that could be repeated and duplicated that took into consideration all the variables we knew ultimately impacted, if a home was SOLD. After thousands of transactions and hundreds of hours, through market research my partner and I identified Seven Laws that impact price elasticity in the real estate market. When identified, they covered all systems, tactics, and strategies that had a positive cause and effect relationship during the home selling process. We have proven that when these Laws are obeyed, the homeowner can sell their home for up to 18 percent more money than traditional methods.

Read the *7 Mistakes Report*. Get the people to read the report.

About Michael

Michael Reese, a Lawton, OK native, started his real estate career approximately 7 years ago, but he's been groomed for sales and excellence his entire life. The son of a Command Sergeant Major, Michael said that in his house, his mother had only one way to do things "exactly and completely – there was no gray area." As a result of this adherence to following through, Michael has excelled in every sales job he's had. In fact, as a teenager, he was asked by his school to not sell the candy his mother bought for him in bulk at the store because he was outselling the school itself and cutting into their profits.

In 2002, after a visit with his friend Jay Kinder, Michael decided that real estate was the career for him. In his first two years in the business, he sold over 100 homes. In his third year alone, he exceeded that two-year total by more than 24 homes. By the end of his 5th year, at only the age of 27, he achieved what most real agents dream of, earning over $1,000,000 GCI in a twelve-month period. By the end of his 6th year, he had sold over 500 homes in his short real estate career and he's on pace to sell almost 250 homes this year.

In 2006, he and his team at Keller Williams were voted the "Best of Business" for Frisco, TX. As well, he was voted a member of the prestigious "30 under 30" group for Realtors across the United States. In 2007, Michael ranked within the Top 5 for Keller Williams in the Southwest Region and currently holds the ranking of #19 worldwide.

Understanding that you get more when you give, Michael regularly speaks to new agents entering the ranks at the Champions Real Estate School in the Dallas area. He values what he learned there and wants everyone to be successful in his or her real estate career. He has also created systems and programs within his real estate business that allow his agents to be successful and still have balance in their lives. These same programs have created a great real estate enterprise that delivers amazing results to his clients.

His philosophy is very simple. He believes that you don't have to be the best Realtor, just the best marketer. The one with the most clients makes the most money. The more people you can get in front of, the better chance you have to sell more homes and the more people you can help.

Michael currently does coaching with Jay Kinder for real estate agents from around the country, and he is in talks to do some training for a variety of organizations nationwide that serve the real estate industry. His goal is to serve others to help them meet and exceed their wildest dreams and expectations.

CHAPTER 3

In Real Estate and Life, It's Not What You Know, It's How You Think

By Brian Combs

Nick is a Realtor I have known many years. He is a true "student" of the real estate industry; he has been to all of the "how to" seminars and countless training events. His home office is packed with scripts, dialogues, presentations, books and strategies used by the top Realtors in the country. Why is Nick broke? Why is Nick struggling in real estate? Do you know Nick? Are you Nick? What happens to the hundreds of thousands of Realtors across the nation each year who attend seminars and walk out ready to light the world on fire? With pages of notes, strategies and "aha" moments, they shout "Finally, the keys to my success!" I am ready! Then…………..nothing is acted upon.

Let's be clear about something; you already possess all of the knowledge needed to make millions in real estate. Stop looking for the "magic pill" that will make you a success. Your lack of taking action on what you ALREADY know is a result of HOW YOU THINK.

Before age 21, I completed my first year in the real estate industry. After closing 65 transactions, I was honored as the National Rookie of the Year for the major franchise I worked with. If you haven't already guessed, neither extraordinary skills nor massive amounts of knowledge contributed to my success. I was still only shaving every 4 days and lived with my parents! How was I able to outsell almost every other agent in my marketplace? …The same way anyone succeeds at anything; a winning mindset.

You can have all the knowledge in the world and it will be useless if you are not thinking the way high achievers think. After all, I know many "professional students" who are flat broke in our industry. This chapter is about getting you into action………… and right now! This is what you want, isn't it?

I. THINKING DICTATES ACTIONS

What do you say to yourself? What do others say and you buy into it? How do you describe your life and business? Henry Ford said, "Whether you think you can or think you can't, either way you are right." Until now, you may not have realized the depth of his brilliance and that of many others who support the power of positive self-talk.

Most people say affirmations. The problem is they are negative affirmations (…I can't, …I am overwhelmed, …this is too hard, …the market stinks), and until you decide to consciously say positive things you will keep getting the results you have been getting. Whatever you say to yourself becomes YOUR reality. Your Reticular Activating System (RAS) will assist you by only bringing to your attention, proof to support your beliefs. What is your RAS? In 1995, I attended a seminar and discovered I had a RAS. So do you. It is part of our brain that only brings to our attention what we have expressed is important to us. Here's an example: You get a new car and immediately begin noticing all of the other cars on the road like yours. Prior to THINKING about getting that car, those same cars were all around and you didn't even notice. If you say buyers are "tire kickers," I guarantee not many are in your car − buying through you. Your brain

(RAS) is busy looking for proof to validate your affirmations. Self-sabotage sets in and each time you meet a new buyer-prospect, sub-consciously you believe they will waste your time, so the effort you put into helping them is minimal at best. Meanwhile, another Realtor is having massive success with buyers, because their self-talk is far different from yours. You've heard "What you think about comes about" haven't you? People and situations show up for you how you expect them to, and will never disappoint you!

STRATEGY FOR SUCCESS:

Make a list of what you say, hear or think regarding:

1. Yourself

2. Sellers

3. Buyers

4. Lead generation/prospecting

5. The real estate market

6. Your loved ones/your life

By writing this down, you will begin realizing what you are affirming to yourself each day and how your focus is on things that are literally crippling your results and relationships. Next, write a new list of affirmations, opposite to what you currently say. You don't have to believe yet; you are simply stating a new way you intend on viewing people, things and situations. Your RAS now works with you by bringing to your attention everything supporting your new thought process. And as you know, new thinking leads to new actions.

Realize you have choices; continue with your current self-talk (please consider the results you are getting) or decide to create new verbiage for how you describe everything in your life. Remember Nick, the young man I described earlier in this chapter? Nick is taking action and getting huge results. Changing his self-talk was a major factor.

II. YOU CANNOT BE, DO OR HAVE
WHAT YOU RESENT

How do you treat phone solicitors? Do you cut them off and rudely hang up on them? How do you react to a mailbox or inbox full of marketing or solicitations? Are you "that" person who says "take me off your stupid list and quit sending me stuff?" When you are dealing with a salesperson closing YOU for a sale, do you become agitated or annoyed? Do you call them pushy? Why am I bringing this up and what does it have to do with your success and mindset? I will make a bold statement coming from my personal experiences working with thousands of Realtors in my lifetime. If your behavior resembles that from above in regards to how you receive promotion, marketing or salesmanship, I can almost promise you something; you are probably struggling to make sales and reach your potential.

Every human being has a desire to look good. Admit this or not, it's true. It's not a bad thing. It just is. Accept it. Because you desire to look good, it is nearly impossible to be, do or have anything you view as *bad*. If you resent "salespeople" you are not closing for sales. If you resent solicitation you aren't promoting your own services. If you resent receiving calls from salespeople you are not on the phone making calls for yourself. And if you are not doing these things how do you expect to be successful in real estate? To take this one step further, I request your total honesty. What have you heard or even said yourself about high achievers? How many times have you been a part of conversation, usually involving broke people, centered on how horrible those 'top producers' are? Greedy, pushy, workaholics, arrogant, no life and manipulative are a few adjectives that far too many non-producers use to describe success. Because you desire to "look good" you won't do what it takes to be successful – so long as you associate this type of negativity with people who are actually amazing!

STRATEGY FOR SUCCESS:

1. Show appreciation and offer thanks to anyone you come across who is promoting themselves, their services and/ or business. The next time you receive a solicitation call, congratulate the caller for doing their work. Tell them you admire their efforts and appreciate them actually having a job. By accepting these calls with gratitude, you will begin to see how others will accept calls from you so you can grow your business as well.

2. Schedule a lunch or coffee every week with someone who is earning double what you earn. You will learn high achievers have many things in common: giving, honesty, ethical, focused, hard-working and they deeply care about helping others. As you notice these outstanding qualities, it will become easy for you to realize how inaccurate you or others have been in describing the wealthy of the world and you will see being a success is not *bad*.

III. SOME WILL......SOME WON'T......SO WHAT!

What is your mindset about being told "No"? Each day the job of a real estate agent is to do what? Generate new business. I realize some of my readers will say your job is customer service and let's be honest; who are you going to provide service to if you have no leads? The obstacle for most agents is failure to accept "no" and "rejection" as part of the process for finding people to serve. Customer service is extremely important; please don't misunderstand what I am saying. My career has been blessed by many things; one is delivering great service and the other is my desire to find lots of people to serve. This section is about changing the way you look at rejection. Let me very nicely tell you something about rejection. I will be as gentle and kind as I can, given the seriousness of this topic. Are you ready? *Build a bridge and GET OVER IT!* That's right, I said it. It had to be said. If you don't like rejection you are perfectly normal. I don't like rejection any more than you do. In fact, I haven't met many top producing salespeople who do enjoy rejection. However, ask them if they are WILLING to be rejected and the answer is HELL YES! Being rejected is nothing compared to being broke. Did you hear that? Ask yourself what hurts worse, being broke or being rejected? Successful people do things they don't enjoy doing because those activities are necessary for the results they seek. Here's a fun story. I was at my buddy's house one day and observed this dialogue between him and his teenage son. My friend told him, *"Mow the yard." His son replies*, "I don't like mowing the yard." *My buddy says*, "First of all, who asked you if you liked it or not, and secondly, what does your liking it have to do with whether or not you will do it?"

Do you get the picture?

Some will, some won't, and so what carried me through my initial struggles in real estate. I suggest you accept today you will hear "no" more than "yes." The key to your breakthrough will be looking at rejection differently, and I will show you how. "No" is a profitable word. Trust me, you can't hear "yes" without hearing "no," just like "hot" only exists because of "cold" and "up" only exists because of "down." Think about your favorite basketball player. They earn $5 million per year and shoot the ball 2,000 times. Do they make every shot? No. When you do the math you see each shot they take is worth $2,500, even when they miss. Does this make the missed shots bad? Of course not. All shots we take are worthwhile and have a value. It is the shots we don't take and the business we don't ask for, that leads to failure.

STRATEGY FOR SUCCESS:

1. Calculate your dollars earned for each "no" you receive. Because you are serious about changing how you think about rejection so in turn you will take different actions leading to improved results, you will need to track your results.

2. Track how many live contacts you make and (by phone or in person) from those contacts, how many buyer/seller contracts you are obtaining. What is your average commis-

sion?

3. For demonstration purposes, let's assume you make 30 contacts and get 1 "yes" and "no" 29 times. What is the "yes" worth? Assume you earn $5,000. By dividing your 30 "shots taken" by $5,000 you realize each shot is worth $166 even when you get told "no." Some will, some won't, so what!

Remember Nick? This fresh outlook on rejection worked for him and thousands of others I have worked with. It will work for you too! Think of rejection like a stack of money on your desk. Each time you make a contact, pull out $166 and put it in your pocket, no matter what the outcome.

IV. IT'S NOT ABOUT YOU

My initial results weren't anything to brag about and I quickly figured out how my thinking was holding me back. Then I went on to close 65 sales as I mentioned earlier. I am grateful to have learned something from others around me and I am going to share it with you. It is worth saying I have passed this advice about "thinking" differently onto many others and now they are succeeding and so will you. In the beginning, I felt greedy and selfish asking for business. As you can imagine I wasn't enjoying prospecting very much. My fear was having people I knew, privately or publicly, resent my efforts and view me as a pest. Then I had one of those "aha" moments!

Buying or selling real estate, for most people, is the biggest financial decision they will ever make. Shouldn't I be thinking about helping them make the wisest choices possible? Shouldn't I be thinking, "How can I help the MOST number of people?" Shouldn't my efforts be all for THEM? And when I make it all about them, serving their needs, their family and their financial future, won't they see how much I care? Will it not be a natural result that I am successful too? Today I see how many Realtors are paralyzed by the same fears I had. Top agents recognize making calls is NEVER about their own personal gains or their money. *Stop thinking about yourself.* Decide now to not concern yourself with looking silly or bothering others, and commit to helping the most number of people have an amazing real estate experience. When I changed the way I was thinking, I never again felt like a bother to anyone and rejection didn't get in my way either. I saw by not asking for business I was not in a position to help anyone, and frankly, that seemed awful.

I care about people. Do you? I have asked countless Realtors "Why did you get into this business?" One answer always comes up, "I love helping people!" Are you sure? How many did you help last year? The majority of agents aren't helping very many people because of how they think. Consider this; if a coffee shop opened and said their mission was to serve as much coffee to as many customers as possible, what would you think of them if they only had five customers all year? If you love helping people, which I suspect is one of the many reasons you got into real estate, please start proving it. How many horrible stories have you heard from buyers and sellers about their negative real estate experiences? There are far too many, don't you think? In our current economy, is it not true buyers and sellers need help like never before? Isn't it true a seller whose listing expired had goals and plans that have been put on hold because a Realtor didn't get the job done? Isn't it a statistical fact most For Sale By Owners end up listing with an agent because they are unable to get the job done themselves? Do you care enough about helping people to reach out to them? Aren't buyers concerned about falling values and making the wrong choice? If you are unwilling to be there for them, who is? Someone with a winning mindset is, because they are truly about helping people and are willing to risk being uncomfortable to do so.

SUCCESS STRATEGY:

Get out your pen and paper. Answer these basic questions.

1. Who do you believe is the best person to help your friends, family and all of their friends, family and co-

workers with their real estate needs – buying and selling? I trust you just wrote: ME (...as in YOU).

2. Do you believe it is important your friends, family and everyone they know make wise decisions about buying and selling real estate? And they should be careful how they spend their real estate dollars?

3. Do you believe it is crucial your friends, family and everyone they know be knowledgeable about the real estate market so they can make wise choices?

4. Who is keeping them informed about the market and entering into dialogue with them about the market and their options so they can make good choices?

If you answered these questions the way I suspect you did, then it becomes apparent IF you TRULY care about people, calling them and seeing how you can help them would become a PRIORITY rather than the CHALLENGE you have been making it.

About Brian

Brian Combs is a professional speaker, coach, master trainer, real estate investor and franchise owner. Organizations across the country employ Brian because of his energetic and passionate way of delivering invaluable techniques and strategies – which literally cause overnight transformations in people and entire companies. Brian has the unique ability to bring a room to tears or laughter while keeping learning and implementing both fun and attainable. Brian's energy and passion for life and helping others is infectious. Anyone who spends time with Brian feels and believes they can accomplish anything they desire in life or business. To get more information about Brian, go to: www.BrianCombs.com or contact him directly at 360-882-2867.

Reference Letter:

I come from 22 years of high-level management and sales with two Fortune 100 companies (Johnson & Johnson and Gillette). Brian Combs was my real estate coach and I was meeting with him after I had heard him speak at a large gathering in the Portland/Vancouver Metroplex. I could not quit thinking of his presentation. It finally occurred to me that Brian had missed his true calling. He was not meant to be in Real Estate at all! His whole life has been preparing him for public speaking. The creativity he had to apply messages to the room was filled with pure brilliance. Very quick on his feet thinking. I do not say that lightly. After 22 years of corporate training, I have heard many of the best speakers out there from Ziglar to Robbins and those in-between. I have forgotten more than most have been exposed to. Not Brian, I continue to marvel at the way he could mold a story and make it memorable.

The next time I met with Brian I said to him, "Brian, you know my corporate background; I have heard the best of the best when it comes to speakers and you are as good as or better than any of them. You belong on a stage." I do not get impressed easily. I have surrounded myself with many incredibly talented individuals and worked with some great Dream Teams. I believe the really great speakers are those that have a passion for what they believe in and walk-the-walk, not just talk-the-talk. Brian speaks and it is hard to find the words to describe the profound impact he has on individuals. He is a gift to all of us fortunate enough to hear him. With my highest regards, Patty Bright

CHAPTER 4

I've Bought and Sold 2,000 Houses. Here's What I've Learned

by Ron LeGrand

One of the most common things people fear about getting into real estate is they're afraid they can't sell the house, and somehow they'll get stuck with it. I can understand why this would create anxiety for a beginner, because they simply don't have enough facts to overcome the fear. However, if you're not a beginner and this is still a problem, there's no excuse for it. So let's get it fixed right now. The truth is… selling should be the easiest part of your business.

Are you not buying because you're waiting to sell what you have first? Is your income suffering because you haven't plugged the hole in the back end? Are you so afraid of selling you quit (or never started) buying?

In this chapter, I'll discuss the reasons why some people have trouble selling and how to fix them. I've identified 14 reasons here. Pay close attention to numbers 4-7 because combined with number 1, they equal about 80% of why houses don't get sold quickly.

Most of the time it's a people problem, not a house problem. So here we go, in no particular order.

35

14 Reasons why houses don't sell quickly:

1. Not ready to sell.
2. Poor area.
3. Overpriced.
4. Salesperson's personality problems.
5. Inflexibility of seller.
6. Salesperson's lack of knowledge about financing programs available.
7. Salesperson's lack of knowledge of funding and prescreening.
8. No follow up system in place.
9. Functional obsolescence.
10. House very small.
11. Salesperson loses control of the loan process.
12. House located too far away from the city.
13. House is in high price range where few buyers can afford.
14. Only one bath.

Notice the majority of these problems are directly related to the person in charge of making the sale...and the rest should be fixed before you buy.

Problem #1 - Not ready to sell

Front appearance - Would you want to see the inside? Is the front attractive, well- landscaped with two colors on house, attractive front door, mailbox and shutters?

Roof - Does it need to be replaced? If so, the house will not sell until its replaced and the lender will require it anyway.

Exterior paint - Is it at least 2 colors and looks fresh? Are the colors pleasing or gaudy?

Interior paint - Is it two colors, or docs it look like a white tornado went through it?

Interior trim - Is there color, paper borders, blinds, bath and kitchen accessories, lever door handlcs, shower curtain or door, etc.?

Carpet - Same old lifeless, ugly brown or have you checked on modern colors? Would you want this carpet installed in your home?

Central heat and air - If you're in the southern two-thirds of the country, it's not an option. Do it.

Kitchen - Does it have plenty of cabinets or just enough to get by? Add all you can and today marble-like counter tops are expected. Stainless steel appliances also help sell.

Customers won't complain about shoddy repairs. They just won't buy. If it doesn't look good enough to satisfy your wife, your buyers won't like it either. Spend a few more dollars and make it a house you can be proud to sell and know your buyer will rave to others about it. Gentlemen, you should not decorate houses or pick colors - you suck at it. Get the ladies to do it and get out of their way.

Is it staged? Make it look like a home, not a box. Rugs, plants, pictures, counter items, blinds, a little furniture. It must smell nice with electricity on. This can be done for a few hundred dollars by ladies only.

Lock box on door with key and another hid on premises.

If you do a good job here, amazing things will happen.

1. It will sell quickly.
2. It will appraise for more.
3. You'll sleep well at night.
4. Your buyers will send you customers.

5. Your good reputation will spread quickly.

6. The neighbors will send you customers or sell their houses to you.

7. Your attitude will improve and you'll enjoy dealing with buyers more because you know you have a great product.

8. You'll save the extra money you spent in holding costs. So, in reality all these benefits are free.

9. It'll probably even improve your sex life. Think about it. More sales means more money. More money means happier spouse or significant other. Happier spouse means more frequent and better sex. I heard that on Oprah the other day.

Problem #2 - Poor area

Is it a war zone? If so, you must learn to sell low income houses, or don't buy there if you intend to retail.

In low income areas it's critical you master the art of financing. You will not survive if all your sales must be to a buyer or sold for 100% cash out.

Problem #3 - Overpriced is not what you think

Just for the record, all my houses are overpriced. And I'm proud of it, in case anyone asks. You should always set your sales price higher than what the house appraised for. If you don't ask for more I can assure you, you won't get it. But there is a limit. You can't go nuts on me here. Putting a $125,000 price on a $100,000 house is pushing the envelope. However, putting a $109,900, or maybe even a $114,900 price on it may work fine.

Your market will tell you quickly. If the buyers all complain about the price, you know you have a problem and you may want to lower it a little.

Warning! Make sure the price is the problem before you go fixing what isn't broke. Only your buyers can tell you the price is too high. Not your spouse, your neighbor, your brother-in-law or even your Realtor. If I had $100 for every time a Realtor told me my price was too high, I'd be in a higher tax bracket. Actually, that's not true. They don't get any higher.

You can always lower the price. You can't raise it once it leaves your lips. I don't know for sure, but I bet I haven't lowered the price on more than 15% of all the houses I've done to get them sold. As a rule, a 5-10% above appraised value or good comps is the upper limit. You'll have to decide the price based on the area, condition, salability and heat of the market. Just don't be giving away money because you're listening to morons.

Problem #4 - Salesperson's personality problems

Have you ever talked to a seller or a Realtor you didn't like? A mean-spirited, grouchy, personality perhaps? How about someone who just won't shut up long enough for you to ask a question? Maybe you've encountered the prescreened type who treats you like the enemy until you pass their qualification test. How about all those times you got the wife on the phone and she was afraid to speak without her husband's permission, or vice versa. That doesn't even count the ones who do talk but never say anything. Then there's the clueless spouse who can't even tell you the asking price, much less the other details.

How about the couple in the middle of a divorce who talk to you like you're the one who just slept with their spouse? Then there's the know-it-all. You know, the kind who wants to do a seminar for you on the phone to impress you with their intelligence in the art of real estate. They can't sell their own house but they can certainly tell you how to do it.

Of course we can't forget all the thinker-brains trying to sell to the reptile-brains, and vice-versa. Or the sellers so in love with their house it takes them 30 minutes to describe every little detail while you're trying to stay awake. Gosh, I'm getting depressed just writing this. I don't want to ever talk to a seller again. Just kidding.

The key for you is not to become like one of those people I just described. If you already are, you can fix it once it's identified. Here's a hot tip. Record your calls and listen to yourself selling your house. If there was a moron on the call you'll probably recognize his/her voice.

Every single time you talk to a buyer you must sound...

Friendly, flexible and excited. If you can't, get someone else to sell your houses.

Problem #5 - Inflexibility of Seller

That means most sellers can only see one way to sell a house, and if that isn't happening the house will sit and sit until that perfect buyer comes along. Finding an A credit buyer to cash you out isn't the only answer. This is especially true for the low-income houses where A+ buyers are scarce.

The more you know about different exits, the easier it will become for you to get flexible. If you don't have your money in the deal and you can live another week without the cash from the sale, it frees you up to get creative and look at other alternatives.

Here's a news flash for you . . .

It's your job to find a buyer who loves your house . . . then make it work!

That means sometimes you must be flexible. It's not a perfect world. Bend a little. Here's a short list of selling methods.

A. Sell to a qualified buyer and cash out now.

B. Lease option and cash out later.

C. Sell with owner financing and help buyer get refinanced later.

D. Sell with owner financing and sell the note at closing or anytime thereafter.

I bet you didn't know you could be that flexible did you? Sorry, I can't go into these in detail here, but I think you get the message. There's always another way.

Problem #6 - Salesperson's lack of knowledge about financing programs available

No, this is not the same thing I just said. If you're going to master your craft of selling houses, you must learn a lot about financing programs. What will kill loans? What programs require little or no down payment? What credit can be fixed and what can't? What will the lender want fixed before closing? Who will let me take back a second and who won't? And 40 or 50 other questions you'll get the answers to as you go.

You don't have to know all there is about financing to sell a house, but the quicker you learn, the easier it gets. Make an appointment with 3 or 4 mortgage lenders and pick their brain. Let them help with what will work and what won't. Then when you get an interested prospect it's simply a matter of getting the buyer's information to the lender of your choice and letting them tell you what will work.

That's the best way I know to learn the ropes about financing. But you know what? A lot of veterans won't even take time to do this. I guess they feel they're too good or too smart to humble themselves and actually ask for help. My friend, what you knew about financing a year ago is not what you should know today. It changes monthly. You must stay on top to be the best.

Problem #7 - Salesperson's lack of knowledge of funding and prescreening.

The first step to success in buying and selling is locating prospects. Without potential buyers it's very hard to sell houses. Frankly, an ad online should be enough to attract plenty of prospects if you know how to write the ad and where to put it. I can't turn this into an ad-writing course, but any ad that gets prospects to call is a good one. Any ad that doesn't is a bad one, or it's in the wrong publication. Make sure your ad gives the prospect a reason to call. Try to include a USP (Unique Selling Proposition): What can you offer that everyone else isn't?

For example:

- Lease Purchase
- No Qualifying Owner Financing
- No Bank Qualification
- No Money Needed
- Easy Terms
- Owner Will Help
- Will Accept Anything On Trade
- You Get A Car With The House, etc.

Some students use flyers distributed in newspapers and don't run ads. Others use a lot of signs, referrals, mail outs, and electronic voice broadcast. We can cover all these in the Quick Start Real Estate School, but the key is to make sure you keep a good flow of leads coming in until the house is sold. Where most people fail is how they handle these leads once they come in.

That, my friend, will receive a lot of attention at the boot camp. It's by far the weakest link in the chain. Leads must be pre-screened properly and the good ones worked daily. Out of any batch of leads will usually come some qualified ones. Maybe not with credit, but qualified if you're flexible as we discussed in the last issue. What I look for most, are people who love the house and are excited about owning it. Give me that and a little something to work with and I'll get them in it.

Problem #8 - No follow up system in place

Why do some folks insist on doing the same job several times when it can be done once? If you're not building a buyer's list of some kind you must love punishment. It's simple. If you have more buyers than houses, you don't run ads, send flyers, mail letters or any of that other stuff. You pick up the phone and call the prospects you've prescreened from the last time and tell them about your new house or simply send an email.

Why is that so hard? It looks to me like it's easier to suffer the pain of creating a buyer's list once, rather than talking to dozens of prospects from ads every time you get ready to sell. You don't have to be an organizational wizard to enact a little follow up. Hey, a pile of prescreened buyers on the corner of your desk with no separation or filing system is better than nothing. Sounds like my system. No, that's not true. At least I put them in a file folder. Then I misplace the folder, but I always know it's close by (somewhere).

Problem #9 - Functional obsolescence

This one is a house problem, not a people problem. You usually can't fix this and shouldn't buy if it's present. That way you won't have trouble selling.

Here are some things that come to mind:

- Extremely small rooms
- Bathroom off the kitchen
- Walk through bedroom to get to the only bath
- Low ceilings (under seven feet)
- House added-on unprofessionally
- Strange layout that can't be fixed
- Adjacent to odors, commercial property, school or anything else that makes it undesirable
- Bad or no foundation

That's just a few of the things I can think of now. Note: Sometimes you can correct this and sometimes you can't. If you don't see a way, simply pass.

Problem #10 - House is very small

I guess this is also functional obsolescence, but it's very common. Any time a house has less than 1,000 square feet I get cautious. I've learned that houses under 900 square foot are usually hard to sell and there's not much you can do but keep looking for a small family of 1 or 2 people. I'm not saying they won't sell. I'm just saying they're harder. I've probably done 200 houses below 1,000 square feet.

I think I own 3 or 4 now. I guess that verifies there is a buyer for every house. If I can buy them cheap enough, I'll still do some today. But I know going in, they may take a little longer to sell.

Problem #11 - Salesperson loses control of the loan process

You must remain in control from the moment you buy the house until you get a check. That includes the loan process. You decide who does the loan, who appraises the house, who gets the survey and termite report and who closes. You are also in charge of speeding up the loan.

Yep! You, not your lender! You should check in every few days, push for results and round up missing paperwork. If you don't, the close will drag on forever. Would you allow your boss to hold your paycheck for 2 to 3 weeks until he decides to pay you? That's exactly what you're doing when you let a loan processor jerk your chain. So, the next time you lose a buyer because he didn't close quick enough, go to your bathroom mirror and cuss out the person responsible.

The last time I lost a buyer two days before closing, it was because God told them not to buy. If I'd been two days earlier, maybe I wouldn't have been competing with God. Oh well. Six weeks later, I sold the house for $3,000 more than the first buyer. Maybe I wasn't competing with God after all.

Problem #12 - House is located too far away from the city

That's an easy one. Don't buy it. Unless you want to create a lot of driving time so you can listen to more of my tapes. Frankly, I don't buy anything I intend to retail that's more than 15 minutes from my office. Of course I know for some of you in big cities that's about three blocks away. Hey, you can always move.

Problem #13 - House is in high price range where few buyers can afford

Actually, sometimes that has no bearing and the high value is not an excuse for a slow sale. The problem is elsewhere on this list. But in smaller cities where a $500,000 house is the mansion, you can certainly expect it to take much longer.

All that just makes a case for you to not guarantee monthly payments on big loans. Unless you're a sadist and looking for pain, you shouldn't try to outguess the market. Don't count on a high-priced house selling quickly just because you like it. Remove the risk, give yourself time and you'll discover the big ones sell just like the little ones, but hopefully with a lot more profit.

Caution!!!

You'd better make sure you have a large spread on those big babies. Buyers of $500,000 and up homes are more sophisticated and more apt to ask for a price reduction.

The good news is these folks can usually qualify for a loan, and the majority of the sales are all cash. Owner financing and lease purchase just doesn't have the sizzle it does on the lower end. That doesn't mean it's not used, only not as often.

Problem #14 - Only one bath

I've sold hundreds with only one bath but it's not my preference. Cheap houses, not a problem. Houses above $80,000 - $100,000, it's very difficult. For houses much above $100,000 it's almost impossible. People who can pay more, want more. If you can't add a bath, you may wish to consider not buying if you feel it's important to the sale.

I have never added a room on the house to add a bath. The only time I have added a bath I've used the existing structure. That should cost you no more than $3,000. Trying to sell a 4-bed/1-bath house ain't easy. Selling a 3-bed/1 bath is okay as long as the house is small. Selling a 2-bed/1 bath is the norm and buyers will expect it.

Well, that's about it. I won't guarantee that every problem you'll run into is on this list, but chances are, the next time you're having trouble selling a house, if you'll take a good look at this list, I bet the problem is in it. If you do run into something out of the ordinary that I've not discussed here, drop me a line.

Here's hoping all your houses sell faster than you can buy them.

In the meantime, remember that there are no real problems, just solutions. And, very often, when you do run across a problem property, there's hidden profit there for someone who knows the answers and can create a solution.

About Ron

Ron LeGrand is a 30 year veteran in real estate with over 2,000 of his own transactions and has trained over 500,000 people in north American on his patented Quick Turn System to buy and sell houses without money, credit, license or experience.

Today Ron runs an active real estate investing business which sells several houses a month, but not like you think. Its not about a long drawn out sales process filled with endless showings and talking to dozens of worthless prospects. It is about a systematic approach getting a few of the right things done to find and pre-screen buyers on autopilot. Combine this with target marketing to attract the right prospects and selling houses should be the easiest part of your business.

Get his free book and CD at www. ronlegrand.com and learn about his live training event at www.RonsQuickStart.com.

CHAPTER 5

Real Estate: The Mindset

By Anita Italiane Hearl

Picture this:

It is a late weekday evening. You walk into a stranger's home. A dog greets you by depositing a smear of saliva on your newly-pressed black slacks while trying to smell your crotch. The husband hits the dog while swearing and takes him outside.

He comes back, crosses his arms and leans back in his dining room chair as he eyes you up and down. The wife is a tad bit more approachable. She states that her husband lost his job six months ago, they haven't been paying their mortgage and they need to sell their house.

Unfortunately, this has been the scene I have walked into more times than not in the past couple of years while selling real estate. Yes, some stories are happy where clients are having twins and need to move into a larger home. Some are buying investment property or are finally able to afford that second home now that prices have dropped dramatically. But the majority of the sellers these days are not taking advantage of this market and are needing to sell.

I can honestly say that every time I walk through that door, I believe that I am the BEST realtor out there and person to help them. I am a professional who knows her market. I know the contracts inside and out, am detail oriented, have a killer marketing campaign and love to negotiate. I possess a great reputation with other agents and do not thrive on ego. But most of all…I love all different kinds of people and genuinely care about the whole person. I thrive on meeting new people, finding out what makes them tick and how to best communicate with them!

Those that know me best say that my compassionate heart is my greatest strength. Because I ruminate and internalize things, sometimes this can also be my biggest source of angst. I remember helping the divorced mom of three young boys sell her home in November. She had accepted an offer from a buyer who was nickel and diming her to the point where through her tears she told me that if she took this offer then she could not buy any presents for her kids this Christmas . We received a back up offer that was considerably higher and it was up to me to get her out of the first offer. I had many sleepless nights wrestling with her dilemma yet was determined to get her out of that first contract. Finding the loophole she needed was a gratifying moment in my real estate career and it did not come easy. We had bosses calling each other, lawsuits threatened, etc. In the end, she sold her house, the boys had a Christmas and we are lifelong friends out of it. I think of her often, and am grateful she entrusted the sale of her home to me!

Home buying and selling is emotional. Some folks are moving towards their dreams….others are having to abandon theirs. People often buy a house because…"it felt like grandmas home!" …or had the same floor plan as when they were growing up. It brought up a feeling…an emotion. Often, there has been a lifetime of living that took place in this home. Dreams were made there, milestones celebrated there, bad news received there. I honor and respect that! I tread lightly there.

Everyone comes to the table with a different life situation. Marriages and individuals are all unique and I love them all. Some want stats, some want you to take control, some are controlling.

Most of the time I will learn more about their finances and situations than close friends and family. One thing is for sure…I know that at the closing of their sale or purchase, I will have earned their trust and have helped them transition to the next chapter of their lives with grace, hope and encouragement. And you know what? Nine times out of ten we will have had fun in the process and become life-long friends.

My four "L" logic tips for successful real estate sales are below: You won't find a system, a marketing plan or the latest "formula." You will find a mindset and a belief that home sales is all about serving the whole person!

1. LOOK! Pay attention. Learn to read people. Queue into their verbal and non-verbal communication and AD-JUST yours.

2. LOOKS! Sellers and buyers rarely meet. When I list a house I represent the sellers. When I present an offer to a seller I represent the buyers. Be the person they are proud to have representing them. Dress up and act professional. This will probably be the largest financial purchase your buyers will ever make and the largest financial sale your sellers will ever do. Treat it as such! First impressions are hard to change.

3. LISTEN! What is motivating them? Being able to hear what they are saying and meeting their needs is HUGE! You are their counselor, coach and advocate. Paying close attention is the way to create value on a number of different levels!

Get into their heads a bit! Sometimes it is NOT about the house. There are times where folks are so caught up in the emotion of a lost dream (divorce, foreclosure, a death), that it is up to me to relay to them that this situation does not define them. This is a blip on the lifeline of their life. There are better times ahead. Help them to focus, take control of what needs to happen, and move on!

4. LEAD! People want clarity and confidence all the way through the process. So take charge, maintain control and keep the momentum going!

In conclusion, it comes down to the ability to maintain one's focus and strike a balance between the client's emotional and financial dynamics while keeping a sure hand on all the details, including guiding the process through the inevitable "bumps along the road" that are part and parcel of any real estate transaction.

About Anita

WHAT'S IN A BRAND?

It's pretty simple....deliver on the experience you've promised.

That approach to real estate sales has resulted in Anita Italiane Hearl being in the top 5% of producers in the Seattle area year-in, year-out, good times and bad, for over 12 straight years. She does what she says she will...and then some...and it's this simple commitment to going above and beyond that sets her apart from the pack – and consistently turns clients into lifelong friends.

WHAT'S IN THE PERSON:

Anita possesses a genuine interest in, and concern for, the wide variety of people she serves and derives great satisfaction in seeing her clients move forward in life, getting from where they are now to where they want to be. Many times this calls on her unique blend of tenacity coupled with a caring, human touch – taking the stress out of what can be one of life's most emotional events.

Anita Italiane Hearl grew up on Mercer Island, attended the University of Washington, has lived and owned property in Portage Bay, Fremont, Green Lake, Whidbey Island and now Sandpoint. She and her husband have raised two daughters in Seattle, and she has gleaned an extensive ("encyclopedic") knowledge of the cities unique neighborhoods, "hot spots," schools and amenities.

BOTTOM LINE:

Best in Client Satisfaction Award by Seattle Magazine (2004-2011).

This says a lot....based on the combination of professionalism and personality, ONE realtor in Seattle was chosen to represent the city on HGTV's "Bang for your Buck" television series for 2011...that was Anita Italiane Hearl!

CHAPTER 6

Protecting Your Assets

By JW Dicks, Esq.

Fair warning: if you are new to real estate, this chapter can be a little scary because it contains a great many words of caution. On the other hand, you might see this chapter as very positive. After all, it's entitled "protecting your assets," rather than "how not to lose your assets."

The main lesson we want to convey in this chapter is that you have to be realistic about being in business (including the real estate business), because there are many things that can go wrong. To protect yourself, you must be vigilant not only when you have a problem, but before you have one. Planning for problems using risk-management strategies is the best way to counter those problems when they do arise – and we always work on the assumption that they will arise.

Advanced Real Estate Strategy No. 1:
SET UP YOUR INVESTMENTS IN LEGAL STRUCTURES THAT OFFER MAXIMUM PROTECTION

The first place for us to start with a protection plan is with your legal structure. Most investors buy investment property in their own name, and they frequently buy it jointly with their spouse. This is a mistake for investment property, because you immediately expose all of your assets and your spouse's assets to problems and lawsuits arising out of this one property. Except for your home and property that you are trying to get financed as a second home, your real estate should be owned through an entity such as a corporation, trust, or limited partnership. The choice depends somewhat on your state law, but we prefer to use a particular type of corporation called a limited liability company, or LLC.

If someone gets hurt on one of your properties and sues you, then you and your personal assets are protected by the corporate shield that owns and "surrounds" the property. No, this does not mean that you won't get sued. Alas, attorneys sue everyone when they file an action for damages, and they try to get as many people as they can involved. It is part of the game, but from your point of view, it isn't a fun game.

Your attorney's job, if it ever comes to that, is to show that you have a properly set up corporation and that if there is any problem, it should be limited to the assets of the company and not involve you personally. If you have kept good corporate records and conducted yourself as we advise in this book, we think that you have little to fear because a corporation is a separate entity. The state government isn't too interested in seeing courts "pierce the corporate veil," because if the corporate veil gets pierced too often and too easily, people will stop using corporations, and then the big fees states earn from corporations will go away. This doesn't mean that a simple incorporation is a 100 percent surefire protector, but it is close.

We also take the corporate protection a step further, using a separate LLC for each property we own. If you put all of your assets into one LLC, then all of those assets are involved in any litigation involving any one of the properties. The disadvantage of the multiple entity approach is cost. But believe us: this is not the area where you want to be saving money. Hire a good lawyer the first time to set up the right type of corporation or LLC to use in your state, and (if you like) tell him to show you how to do it yourself from then on, so that you can save the fee. Again, though, we don't usually cut corners when itcomes to buying expert professional help.

We use LLCs instead of "regular" (or "C" or "straight C") corporations because you can elect to use individual tax treatments (for a single-owner LLC) or be treated as a partnership for multiple-owner LLCs. LLCs are relatively new in the corporate world, and some professionals still use a Subchapter S corporation. We like the ease of using LLCs, and there are some benefits that we think make them preferable.

Please Note: Florida has just passed new legislation that decreases the protection of single member LLC's. If you are doing business in Florida, I would either add another partner for a small interest in the LLC or just understand that you won't have protection from creditors you owe for other debts.

One powerful benefit of LLC's, (except for single member LLC's in Florida per note above), is that the stock isn't subject to attachment in civil lawsuits; instead, any plaintiff will be awarded a charging order against the assets. This allows you to continue to operate the corporation, and you can decide not to distribute income to the partners. Since you could continue this method of operation forever, it generally results in settlement discussions between you and the person who sued you, because he won't be getting distribution. You can also structure different classes of stock for different roles and participation. For instance, class A stock could have all voting rights and class B stock just investment returns. You can also use classes of stock to structure preferred returns to one group of investors over another. In short, LLCs are very flexible, and are ideal for structuring investments.

If you decide to make real estate a business instead of just an investment, you will want to form a separate LLC for the business. The reason, as before, is to separate assets and insulate liability for each entity. Your real estate operation with multiple properties might look like this:

Real Estate Property

Each of the properties and businesses has a separate legal structure, and you and whoever you are in business with own the shares or interests in the LLCs. This structure also allows you to own some of the LLCs with different people.

Some advisers may suggest putting all of your interest in these separate LLCs in another LLC that forms a holding company. This is possible, but it does have some potential holding company tax issues. You should consult with your own attorney or tax adviser. It also creates the potential for the holding company to be sued, and that would put all of your assets in jeopardy. In general, our preference is to use separate structures rather than a holding company.

Advanced Real Estate Strategy No. 2:
USE INSURANCE TO PROTECT ASSETS

After the legal structure you operate under, insurance is your second line of defense. Like most things that are worthwhile, insurance is expensive. Someone (the insurance company) is stepping up and saying that for a small amount of money in the form of an annual premium, it will take some of your liability and potential worry off the table. Let the company do it!

You cannot afford to be without insurance. Your only decision is, how much of the risk are you willing to take on in the form of self-insurance? This means deciding how much of a deductible you are willing to accept. The higher the deductible, the higher the risk to you but the lower the cost of the premium. This risk quandary is the essence of the insurance predicament. You are always doing a risk reward analysis, and the equation is a guess at best.

From a practical standpoint, the insurance company makes the risk analysis a little easier because any policy with a deductible of $500 or below will be too expensive for the difference in what you get for the price. Insurance companies do not want to deal with small claims ($500 or less), because they aren't worth the time for the companies to go through the process. So to keep you from making them, they make low deductibles very expensive. Deductibles between $500 and $1,000 are also high, but are more palatable. In this range, people start wanting insurance protection, and policies usually get written in this range as people balance price against reward and risk. The advice to you from this analysis is to check the insurance out at all prices and see where you think the balance comes into play for you.

What Type of Insurance Do You Get?

For most property, the big three are

1. Hazard

2. Wind

3. Flood

To those three, you can add

4. Specialty

5. Title

6. Umbrella

What Does Hazard Insurance Cover?

Hazard insurance is your basic protection against fire, theft, some wind, some rain, and liability. We added the "some wind" and some rain" not as a joke, but because you don't really know how much you are getting until you read the policy. Not everything is covered, and we know that only because we have had a bad experience finding out that "rain" that is blown in by wind is different from rain that comes in because the roof over your head gets a hole in it. Sometimes one is covered and the other is not, and sometimes the deductibles are different. The problem is, you have to read your policy, or you have to ask, to know what type of protection you want. By the way, you want both, but you may have to buy two policies to get them.

An additional problem with insurance contracts is that even if you ask what the policy says, policies change. Remember all of those pesky little addendums to your contract that you get in the mail - the ones that most of us throw away? Next time, read one. You will be surprised, because they are the very things we need to understand. Ask questions regarding coverage and deductibles as well and as often as you can. This is why a good insurance agent is worth the fee you pay.

Are All Wind Policies the Same?
The answer to this question, as you may already suspect, is a resounding no. Even if wind is included in a basic policy, it includes neither hurricane wind nor tornado. You have to have a special clause and coverage for those. What happens if the wind knocks over the kerosene lantern you have burning in your house so that you can read, your neighbor gets hurt when the fire starts, and he knocks over the toilet bowl, flooding the property? Which of your insurance policies is going to pay off? The answer (before you even try to guess) is, who knows? All we can tell you is that the great insurance contract drafters in the sky will have a formula to apply, and it will probably cost you more.

Flood Insurance
Premiums for flood insurance policies in areas that are hurricane prone or below flood plain elevations are very expensive. In Florida, we have such a difficult time with this that there is a special state insurance fund to cover certain policies. Many insurance companies have lost so much money writing policies that they have left the state. The remaining companies were charging premiums that were almost unaffordable, so the state had to step in. There were good reasons for the state to intervene. Without the state fund, buying and selling beachfront property would have

come to a standstill. Many people swore that they would start "going naked" (meaning having no insurance), but they forgot the clause in their mortgages requiring insurance. The lenders started writing nasty little letters saying, "Get insurance, or we will get it for you at an even higher price, and add it to your mortgage. If you don't pay, then we'll default you."

The bottom line is that you have to get flood, wind, and other insurance coverage if you're going to get a property that has a loan on it, so you'd better plan to shop around for the best deal. Often you have to shop each year at renewal time, because rates go up substantially once the "teaser" rate year expires.

What Is Specialty Insurance?

Specialty insurance can be many things. Earthquake insurance is one example. Special riders for certain personal property that you want protected under your homeowner's plan, such as your expensive watch or ring, can be another. sometimes you aren't told about what is available in the form of additional riders, so you need to ask. Sometimes the additional riders are so expensive that you decide to self-insure. As long as you self-insure with a true understanding of the trade-offs involve, that's fine. We rarely do add-ons for jewelry or other personal property, but we know people who do and who sleep better at night because of it. If that is you, go for it.

Title Insurance

As we have previously discussed, title insurance protects the policyholder against any title problems for which the title insurance policy has not made an exception. And that is the rub, because these policies make exceptions for most things. You as the buyer must always take it upon yourself to review the exceptions noted and get them stricken from the policy. In most cases, you can do this except for ones that are standard, such as the exception for "any recorded instruments." Recorded title instruments can be read by you or your attorney in advance, so you can decide when you see them whether or not they are important. Except for those, you really don't want exceptions.

Your lender will always get a title policy to cover property you buy. You will also pay for this policy, so read it as well. If the title insurance doesn't protect the lender, you will have to pay to correct any problem that arises, so see if you have any insurance backup. Don't forget to also ask the title company to give you a discount for writing the lender's policy. The seller will have to give you a policy when you go to closing for the full protection of the property, so you should get credit on the second policy, because it really cover only problems over and above what was covered under the owners. This discount is common practice, but only if you ask for it. So ask. (Note that in some states buyers pay for both title policies.)

Advanced Real Estate Strategy No. 3: <u>GET AN UMBRELLA POLICY</u>

The umbrella policy is a blanket policy that insures and protects You, not your real estate, for anything you haven't been covered for, liability-wise under any other policy you hold. If, for example, a problem develops on one of your properties and the liability claim is larger than your homeowner's or hazard insurance policy, your umbrella insurance would kick in to protect you for the balance. The umbrella policy is inexpensive (a few hundred dollars per year) in light of its huge added protection, and we think everyone should have one. The best place to buy your umbrella insurance policy is where you buy either your homeowner's insurance or your car insurance.

You will find, if you haven't already, that insurance companies give substantial discounts to clients who place all of their insurance with the same company, so it pays to bundle things up and take advantage of the discounts. As long as you are asking for discounts, it also pays to ask your agent if there are any other discounts that you might qualify for, such as a senior citizen's discount.

Advanced Real Estate Strategy No. 4:
BE PREPARED WITH A LEGAL DEFENSE STRATEGY

The more you have, the more someone is going to want to take it away from you. In addition to the fact that real things can go wrong and unfortunate accidents can occur on your properties, there will also be people who try to take advantage of you simply because they think you have more than they do, and somehow that is wrong. In both cases (the legit and the not-so-legit), you are going to be involved in a lawsuit. Lawsuits cost you in both time and money. The best defense is a good offense, and you will have to have an attorney to be your quarterback.

There are two ways to deal with the legal system. One is by hiring the best law firm for the type of problem you have, and the other is to use a form of insurance called prepaid legal services. Depending on the size of the case, you may have no choice but to get the best attorney you can find. On the other hand, prepaid legal services are a relatively easy way to handle initial problems that may go away if the other side concludes that you are going to be serious about defending your position. With prepaid legal services, you are given the telephone number of a prequalified attorney to speak to about your type of problem. Telephone calls are for the most part completely covered under the plan, for about $25 per month.

Additionally, you can have a legal letter written for no additional charge, and sometimes that is all that is necessary to let people know that you're serious. Should the case escalate, you will get a discount on additional legal services, including going to court. If you like the attorney and are comfortable with her qualifications, sticking with her at discounted rates may be a good idea. On the other hand, at this point, you are also free to go out and hire someone else. The point is that the relatively modest sum of $25 a month covers you for some early legal forays, and it gives you a name and a firm to throw out to the other side when you say, "Hey, call my lawyer."

Advanced Real Estate Strategy No. 5:
OPERATE YOUR BUSINESS LEGALLY

A number of people in real estate (as in all businesses) don't always do things the right way. You will meet people who say, "It really isn't necessary to get a building permit to do that small a job." Or, when they talk about disclosures to people you are dealing with, "Don't worry; what they don't know won't hurt them." You can always choose to find an ethical dilemma in a complicated situation. We encourage you not to find the dilemma. Don't cut corners. Tell people the truth. In the long run, it will serve you well.

Sure, it may seem that people are getting away with things that you aren't, and your stance may even cost you money in the short term. But we're convinced that over the long term, sleazy behavior catches up to people. In addition to the fact that such behavior is just wrong, we believe that it also exposes you to risks that will, if nothing else, complicate your life unnecessarily. In short, if you need a building permit to do some work, get a permit. If something needs to be disclosed, disclose it. Always dealing with people in an aboveboard way will gain you a reputation for being the kind of person people want to deal with. You will have more deals brought your way, and people will tend to treat you the way you are known to treat others. Sure, there will be some people who will try to take advantage of you, and we aren't suggesting that you let them do so.

Just do what you are supposed to do, and, again, don't cut corners: legal, ethical, or whatever. Don't expose yourself to risks just to do something that may be faster or more profitable in the short term. It's almost always too expensive in the long term-and you're in real estate for the long term.

THE ASSET-PROTECTION CHECKLIST

(i) GET THE RIGHT LEGAL STRUCTURE IN PLACE.

There are lots of different ways to structure your business. Look into your options, and get good counsel. The general rule is to shield the assets in one corner of your life from trouble in other corners of your life.

(ii) GET ALL THE INSURANCE YOU NEED (AND THEN SOME).

All right, maybe not "and then some." But insurance, by and large, is cheap. It can buy you great peace of mind. Just read the fine print, and don't assume anything that you read there is nonnegotiable. Negotiate!

(iii) DO IT LEGALLY.

By this we mean two things. First, set up your legal defenses so that you look like a porcupine - not worth tangling with. And second, stay well within the spirit and letter of the law. Do things right. If it smells, looks, or sounds bad, stay out of it. You'll sleep better. You'll prosper.

About JW

JW Dicks, Esq. is an attorney, best-selling author, entrepreneur and business advisor to top Celebrity Experts. He has spent his entire 35-year career building successful businesses for himself and clients by creating business development and marketing campaigns that have produced sales of over a billion dollars in products and services. His professional versatility gives him a unique insight into his clients' businesses to see untapped opportunities to capitalize on, allowing him to use his knowledge of how to structure and position their business to take advantage of them.

He is the Senior Partner of Dicks & Nanton P.A., a unique membership-based, legal and business consulting firm representing clients who want to expand their business. JW helps his clients position their business and personal brand to take advantage of new vertical income streams they haven't tapped into, and shows them how to use associations, franchises, area-exclusive licensing, coaching programs, info-marketing, joint ventures, and multi-channel marketing to take advantage of them.

In addition to consulting and mentoring clients, JW is also a successful entrepreneur and America's leading expert on personal branding for business development. He is co-founder of the Celebrity Branding Agency, representing clients who want to get major media coverage, marketing and PR, and position themselves as the leading expert in their field. His Best-Selling book, *Celebrity Branding You!,* is in its third edition and new editions are currently being published for specific industries. He also writes a monthly column for Fast Company Magazine's Expert Blogg on personal branding, and has written hundreds of articles, blogs and special reports on the subject.

JW has led national conferences and conventions and has spoken to over 160,000 business leaders on branding, business joint ventures, capital formation, investing, and legal and business growth strategies. He is the Best Selling author of 22 business and legal books – including *How to Start a Corporation and Operate in Any State (a 50 Volume set), Celebrity Branding You!, Power Principles for Success, Moonlight Investing, The Florida Investor, Mutual Fund Investing Strategies, The Small Business Legal Kit, The 100*

Best Investments For Your Retirement, Financial CPR, Operation Financial Freedom, Game Changers, How to Buy and Sell Real Estate, Ignite Your Business Transform Your World, and more.

JW is the editor and publisher of The Celebrity Experts® Insider, delivered to clients in over 15 countries, and serves as the guide for entrepreneurs and professionals who are leading experts in their field. He has been called the "Expert to the Experts" and has appeared in USA Today, The Wall Street Journal, Newsweek, Inc. Magazine, The New York Times, Entrepreneur Magazine, and on ABC, NBC, CBS, and FOX television affiliates. Recently, JW was honored with an Emmy nomination as Executive Producer for the film, *Jacob's Turn.*

JW's business address is Orlando, FL and his play address is at his beach house where he spends as much time as he can with Linda, his wife of 39 years, their family, and two Yorkies. His major hobby is fishing, although the fish are rumored to be safe.

CHAPTER 7

Benefits of Home Staging

By Megan Morris

The strongest benefit to staged homes is that they sell for more money in a 'hot' market, known as the seller's market, and sell faster in a slow market, known as the buyer's market or down market. Staging always works to a seller's advantage. If the housing market is sluggish, staging will give your home an attractive edge over the competition. If the market is strong and the home will sell regardless, you can use staging to increase the selling price.

Also, staged homes have curb appeal. As the saying goes in real estate, "You cannot show them the house if you cannot get them out of the car." Plus, if you want your home to peak the interest of potential buyers, the picture on the MLS must stand out. It is estimated that 3 out of 4 people search the internet when looking for real estate. Curb appeal can be a click away when buyers are looking for homes.

Also, landscaping is a very important aspect of curb appeal. In fact, a recent *SmartMoney* article stated that landscaping could add up to 15 % to a home's value. The National Association of Realtors President, Walt McDonald of Riverside, CA was quoted in the article as saying, "When people ask me how they can get strong interest in their property, I always tell them to fix up their landscaping. If a homeowner is reluctant to do it, I tell them they won't get top dollar." Staging prepares a home to stand out from the competition by making it spectacular and memorable.

Staging can be done by the homeowner by following the steps outlined in this chapter, but there are also times when bringing in a professional stager might be helpful. An article in the Nob Hill Gazette's real estate section wrote about a huge benefit to the seller, "Selling a house is always going to be stressful. Quite apart from the logistics involved, the emotions connected with marketing a home where you have lived for years and perhaps even raised a family, can make the process exhausting and even painful. A professional stager, looking at the house with an objective eye, can provide a much needed buffer for many sellers, enabling them to concentrate on settling into their new home."

Home buyers often do not have the vision of how a home could look and they may pay more for the property when they see what they like. Stagers are trained, as you will be too, to see a seller's house through the buyer's eyes. Specifically, staged homes attract the widest audience of viewers, targeting the potential home buyer. Staged homes are also more appealing and are known as the best properties to see. Buyers generally do not buy for potential. They want "move–in" condition property. In addition, staged homes maximize the best features of a house and minimize its faults. Every home has special features and stagers know how to highlight them so the buyers really take notice. What we strive for is to create an emotional "love-at-first-sight" response. It is interesting how many people start house-hunting in a very logical state of mind, but ultimately they buy a home for emotional reasons. Staged homes arouse the powerful feeling: I belong here.

One way stagers define an area of special interest is by making it more interesting. For example, by creating picture perfect arrangements, the eye can be lead to a focal point. You can define a stairway and bring it to life by using wall space in one artistic swoop of picture arranging. Let the stairs guide you. Remember to keep the pictures, paintings or decorative pieces at eye level. It feels more comfortable for people at standard height. By using the banister as a vertical guidepost, stack a pair of prints in the landing, but not to overpower the staircase.

Also, every room needs a purpose and that leads us to form. Form must follow function. Even if you are using the dining room as a nursery, we have to stage it as a dining room. After you have determined what the room is going to be used for and by whom, then the other design elements can be applied. Also, minimize decorating accessories that do not have a function. If you do not need it, pack it and just keep out a few things.

Proportion and scale are important to the overall staging process as well. Proportion is the relation of one part of an object to the whole. For example, if we want to highlight the pool or lake, we might use a lower grouping of furniture to accentuate the view. Select and plan correct proportion to create a comfortable feeling of continuity. There should be very basic pieces in each room so the buyer does not have to think about what else to do with the space. We want the buyers to imagine their furniture in the home as well as giving them decorating ideas.

Keep in proportion; line, color, form and textures within a room. Superfluous or understated emphasis of any design element will be unfavorable within the room. We do not want to put emphasis on any one design element, it should be *subliminal.* The scale of the size of an object to another object must be considered. The scale of an object to the size of the room or area must also be considered. Use of mirrors can add depth to a small room and makes it appear larger. Mirrors can also accentuate a design feature or formalize a room.

Here are some staging tips for bedrooms in your house:

• *Bedrooms should have the basics, look warm and inviting –*
  not cluttered

- *Consider the bedroom angle to offset small rooms*
- *Gender neutral*
- *When walls, carpet and bathroom tile are already pink or blue – go with it and make it a boys or girls room. (Although if it is just paint on the walls, consider painting it neutral)*

Staging a home also incorporates emphasis and focal points. Emphasis is the focal point within a room, used and needed to relieve monotony. In staging we use focal points to draw attention to a part of the house we want the buyer to notice. A focal point could be a beautiful painting, a vertical statue, an arrangement of flowers, an interesting architectural area, a fireplace, etc. The vertical focal points can lead the eye upwards to crown moldings. Decorate the room to flow to the focal point, which holds the most emphasis. We also like to guide the eye around the room like an artist will do in a painting.

Every room should have a main center of interest, in addition to a secondary center of interest in other areas of the room. Remember we are emphasizing the room, not the stuff in it. By following some of these principles, you can see what goes through the minds of stagers.

Use exciting patterns, pieces, and accessories, contrasting in line, shape, texture or color to help create your focal point. When selling the view: *Keep decorating minimal and the windows clean. Remove heavy drapes or tie back so the view is the focal point.*

A well-staged home is also balanced. Balance comes in two forms: symmetrical or even balance, and asymmetrical, or uneven balance. When staging, we usually use a symmetrical landscape to be comforting to the eye. Uneven balance usually creates a more interesting relationship, and is great for emphasizing focal points. Odd numbers of decorative accessories are more interesting than even numbers. When using a floral display, we will usually use three or five stems for a basic arrangement. Even balance can be achieved by placement of the same amount of relative mass, color, and weight on each side. You do not need to use identical items.

Balance, like the focal point, guides the eye and makes the buyer feel comfortable. Objects or color equal in mass will balance each other. Placing mass on one side without placing it on the other, or in a lesser amount, will create asymmetrical balance. Equal amounts of mass or weight on both sides creates symmetrical balance. Always balance opposite walls within a space or room. When staging, we will sometimes put a large mirror on one wall, and a grouping of artwork on the other.

Harmony and unity work hand-in-hand when staging a house. The furnishings and their corresponding elements should appear as if they were planned to be together. Harmony is achieved when variety and unity are combined in a favorable manner. It is important to keep traffic flow in mind when grouping furniture, allowing people easy access to each room. Unity is pulling everything together in a harmonious manner. It is using your palate of staging elements to create your "painted canvas" or well-staged home. Each part added together makes a whole. When a home is well-staged, it is whole, and feels right.

Lines also have function within staging a home. Try to use consistency in the lines within the space. Use one type of line predominately. Vertical lines are masculine, calm and give height. Combined with horizontal lines, things appear classical and strong. Curved lines have personality, rhythm, are active, and look romantic. They tend to be more feminine. Keep these in mind when adding your focal points. If the home is predominantly decorated like a bachelor pad, consider using curvy sticks in an arrangement and add flowers. In contrast, if the home is more on the feminine side, bring in a contemporary sculpture, an arrangement with linear sticks, etc.

There are other elements to think about when creating a staged home. Keep the rhythm and repetition in mind to appeal to the flow of the home. The flow of the pace in a room is the feeling or rhythm. Rhythm is created by using line, spaces, form, colors and patterns with the movement of lines, and by progression, the use of forms from small-to-large or vice versa. It is also the movement, flow, and repetition of colors, patterns and forms around the room. Patterns should be both pleasing to the eye and an accent. For bedding and accessories, we generally will use vertical stripes in a large room and horizontal stripes in a smaller room. Of course this is just like fashion, stripes seem to make one look taller or wider depending which way they go!

Also, use one dominating pattern within the room. Again, if using a pattern, make sure it does not compete with the view or architectural elements we are trying to show off. Also, all patterns used together should coordinate. Make sure there is not too much going on. It is better to have a few pieces that work together than a collection that clashes.

Contrast also creates interest, but remember to use it in a way to draw attention to an architectural area or help guide the eye. We want the home to stand out from the competition, but still fit into the neighborhood.

Another aspect that sets a staged home apart from other homes on the market is the flow of traffic patterns. Traffic patterns should move around conversation areas, not through them. You should be able to walk through the room easily, maybe more easily than a typically-decorated home. For example, when decorating, accent tables are used often to allow comfort for everyone in the seating area. In staging, we would remove some of the accent tables and unnecessary pieces. We use less furniture so the flow of traffic is wider and the buyers can envision their items fitting in. We also want more space for wheelchair accessibility and big families coming through the house.

Staging is an emotional process. It is a big project to declutter and remove all of your personal items from a house that you have created memories in with your family and friends. The most important thing is to keep your ultimate goal in mind – you want to sell your house quickly. Staging helps make the home appeal to everyone and will give you a competitive edge in the real estate market.

About Megan

Megan Morris is the founder of MHM Professional Staging Inc., a successful Home Staging, Décor and Events company in Orlando, and has worked in home staging and design for the past 10 years. In this capacity, she has been responsible for promoting business, managing a team of employees, monitoring projects and customizing client needs on an ongoing basis. Her expertise in visual displays and space planning has been recognized and honored in several design competitions, and she has been hired as the lead set decorator for several commercials, including Nike, Werthers,VH1, New York Life and ESPN.

Her exclusive event company specializes in providing top quality, unique event experiences for her clients. Past clients include The Orlando Convention Center, celebrities, professional athletes, Fortune 500 companies and even international royalty. She was a partner in the launch of the Christian Audigier golf line and was responsible for the kickoff event. Her background also includes marketing and merchandizing when she worked for several department store chains including Nordstrom, Macys and Polo.

Megan is a co-author of the best selling book *TRENDSETTERS*, released in the Fall of 2011, and was nominated for a Golden Quill Award. She has also been featured on FOX News, CNN, MSNBC, HGTV, Bravo and CNBC as an expert in her field. Megan holds a bachelor's degree from the University of Southern California. She is a member of NAWIC, National Association of Women in Business and National Association of Women Business Owners. She is a member of Junior League and is involved in several other philanthropies.

CHAPTER 8

Creating a Recession-Proof Marketing Strategy

David Carroll & Gary Martin Hays, Esq.

Like most real estate agents, your goal is to connect with new clients. Not just with any clients, but those who are ready, willing, and able. These are the active home buyers and sellers who can close in any given market. You have a desire to extend your market reach to connect with people beyond those you already know. As you work with clients actively buying and selling today, you also want to incubate those who *will* be ready in one, six, or twelve months. Above all, you want to create a recession-proof marketing strategy that will allow you to consistently close and thrive in even the worst of market conditions.

To accomplish this, you need to increase your average number of closings per month while targeting the highest commission rates possible. This requires a marketing strategy that queues up more qualified clients than you are capable of managing. Once you exceed the number of clients you can manage, you can selectively focus on the higher commission opportunities while referring the rest to other agents. Sounds easy enough, right?

Eager to get started, you may have created a website that has a property search with registration support. Traditionally, you've been trained to collect as many contact names, emails, and phone numbers to build your lead database. So, your strategy is to capture as many registrations as possible. The problem is you're getting very little traffic to your website. Of those visiting, few are submitting their personal information. Of the few registrations you do collect, you still need to qualify whether the contact is "real" and if they are able to buy or sell today.

Perhaps you've already experienced this problem and began exploring various options for increasing your website traffic. Before long, you've invested countless hours researching and learning about SEO, social media, and online lead generation. Yet, you've only begun experimenting with the many tools, online services, and technologies available to you. Like so many others, you begin to suffer from massive information overload, feeling incredibly overwhelmed and confused. At this point, you still have no clear path for how these tools can improve your business. Worst of all, you're starting to doubt whether or not you have what it takes to be a successful fulltime real estate agent.

If you can relate to any of these statements, you're not alone. Most real estate agents struggle with these same challenges. However, you might be better off than you realize. Where most will simply give up, you have the opportunity to hit the reset button, clear your mind, and start over with a fresh approach. Rather than starting with technology to develop your strategy, start with concepts familiar to you when connecting with new clients face-to-face. Incorporate those points into the way technology should be used in your marketing strategy. The key is not to allow technology to change the way you engage on a personal level. Rather, the way you engage on a personal level should be amplified by technology. This mindset is paramount when developing your recession-proof marketing strategy.

ONLINE NICHE BRAND MARKETING: NEW APPROACH TO EXPANDING YOUR MARKET REACH

Online niche brand marketing is a strategy to expand your market reach within a niche community to capture, engage, qualify, and convert highly-targeted strangers into clients.

Creating a website to collect registrations is not a strategy. It's activating some tools to collect information. It doesn't address the questions of how to increase awareness, establish credibility, engage with community, or qualify your traffic. Online niche brand marketing changes the focus from registrations to engaging with the community. The approach is to capture the core qualities that allow you to successfully connect with clients and apply it to your online strategy. To understand how this works, let's explore this further starting with some basic concepts.

EXPANDING YOUR MARKET REACH TO STRANGERS

Strangers are people outside of your circle of influence. You've not met these people and they know nothing about you. Until strangers are aware of your services, they will remain outside of your reach. The biggest challenge you and other agents struggle with is expanding your market reach to active home buyers and sellers unfamiliar with your services. To understand the most effective way to expand your market reach, let's review the simplicity of how this works in the next scenario.

A STARBUCKS STORY: BEST PRACTICES FOR MARKETING ONLINE

Imagine waiting in line at Starbucks to order your Grande Skinny Vanilla Latte, two pumps, no whip. You overhear a couple behind you talking about a home for sale they were about to check out. Apparently, they found the listing online and were curious about the house and the neighborhood. They appeared to be unfamiliar with the area and were trying to figure out how close they were. At the risk of revealing you were eavesdropping on their conversation, the urge is too strong to resist introducing yourself. You say something to the effect of, "Hi. I couldn't help overhear you asking about this neighborhood. It's located just 3 miles from here. I'm a real estate agent and I'm very familiar with that community." Intrigued by the random occurrence, the couple explains they are expecting their third child and it's time for a bigger home. They also wanted to move into a better school district that isn't too far from where they work. The conversation continues and before you know it, you're showing the home.

What makes this scenario interesting isn't how you would engage if this happened at Starbucks. The point of sharing this story is to review the conditions that made this scenario an opportunity to connect with a stranger, and compare how this can work online.

First, you qualified the couple was searching for homes online and found one they were interested enough to visit. However, there was so much you did not know. Were they working with an agent? What is their time frame to buy? Would purchasing be contingent on selling their current home? Do they need to put their current home on the market as well? Or are they first time home buyers? Will they qualify for a mortgage? How much?

Notice there was no mention of needing to know their name or their phone number or email address? In fact, you probably would never consider saying, "Hi. I'm a real estate agent and I'm familiar with this neighborhood. If you give me your personal contact information, I'll be more than happy to tell you more about this property." The couple would have instantly become guarded and concerned you might be slightly unstable. They certainly wouldn't feel comfortable providing their personal contact information to a stranger. Can you blame them? You've not yet offered them any reason to trust you. *Credibility cannot be established until you share some information that provides value and shows your knowledge and experience.*

Next, you engaged by offering a little information about the neighborhood and indicated you were familiar with the community. You waited for them to ask more questions to further qualify their interest. The more they shared about themselves, the more connected you were getting. This approach makes it much easier for you to ask the questions you needed answered and then request their contact information. If the conditions were right, you could move forward with converting the couple into becoming your client. *Essentially, you engaged in a manner that allowed you to qualify their interest while establishing more credibility.*

Engaging to qualify interest and establish credibility is essential for any online marketing strategy to be successful. However, most agent websites serve merely as online brochures than a device for engaging with their niche community. In the Starbucks scenario, this would be like doing nothing more than handing the couple a business card and asking them to call you later. Without engaging to establish credibility, the couple will most likely not give you a call. Since you did not engage, you can't know for sure if you lost an opportunity to work with a new client.

OPPORTUNITIES IN SOCIAL MEDIA

Conversations like these happen all the time on social media. People are always posting on Facebook, Twitter, and FourSquare where they are and where they're going. This type of chatter persists over time and can be searched.

SIMPLE CASE STUDY: USING TWITTER TO CONVERT A STRANGER INTO A CLIENT

Imagine a college friend posted the message on Twitter:

> *"RT @captaindad I know more about LAX airport than I do about places to live there. Relocating is a pain. – Miss you guys already."*

The fictional message above indicates your college friend "retweeted" (or shared) a message from her friend @captaindad and appended a note indicating she was going to miss them when they moved. Anyone following your friend on Twitter would be able to see her messages, including you.

What would you do if you saw this message? This is pretty much what happened to an agent we know. When she saw a similar message retweeted by her friend in another state, she checked out the profile of the guy moving. She learned he was a pilot out of Houston, TX being relocated to her city. The agent sent a tweet to the pilot suggesting which area of town to check out and the schools to focus on. His response led to a phone call. Just like that, the agent connected with a stranger from another state after qualifying the opportunity, engaging, and finally converting into a client.

NICHE CONTENT: POWERING YOUR CREDIBILITY, MARKET REACH, AND OVERALL SUCCESS

Your niche content is the glue that ties your entire marketing strategy together. It establishes you as an authority in your specific market niche. The content itself is a reflection of your personality, your brand, your experience, and your knowledge of the community. It determines your professional credibility with home buyers and sellers. The amount of search engine traffic you get is determined by the relevancy and credibility of your niche content. It sets the context on how you engage with your community on your website, in social media, and in your email newsletters. The quality and authenticity of your niche content determines your market reach and overall success.

Creating your niche content is simpler than you think. First, identify your niche focus. Maybe you specialize in a specific neighborhood, community, or school district. Maybe your niche focus is active adult living communities, condos in town, or lakefront properties. Incorporate references to your niche focus in everything you write about. If you are writing about a holiday event being hosted in a subdivision, include the subdivision name, the city, or the county. Include landmarks or community features people associate with homes in this subdivision. Maybe it's a golf community or it's near a river or lake. Work these references into the article. Be reasonable and don't overdo it. Make it flow naturally into your content.

Create a list of content categories your community would be interested in. Some examples include neighborhood calendar, school events, concerts in the park, reviewing your favorite restaurants, local market stats, mortgage news, featured properties, and real estate advice. Notice the mix of categories targeting the community, as well as real estate. Don't limit yourself by only targeting those who can be clients today. Your knowledge of the community and your profession should also appeal to a secondary market of followers. These are the people not interested in selling or buying anytime soon. However, connecting with this secondary market of followers will expand your network for future clients and new referrals.

Focus specifically on topics you would discuss with clients. Often times, it's the advice you find routine that your clients find brilliant. Recall all the great advice you routinely share with clients. Some advice is specific to selling in a down economy. Other advice will coach buyers in qualifying for a mortgage. What kind of advice you would give when the home inspection reveals termite problems the sellers were not aware of? How are foreclosures in a neighborhood going to affect a seller's property value? What advice have you shared with staging a home? Should a seller pay high costs on repairs to attract more buyers? These are just a few of the many kinds of advice you've given clients in the past. Turn your great advice into information pages on your website. It is this type of information that will reinforce your expertise, your niche, and your credibility to convert strangers into clients.

Remember, your niche content doesn't have to be overtly focused on real estate. Be creative. We have a friend who focuses his niche on car enthusiasts. The reason is car enthusiasts typically need large garages. And with that comes larger homes. So it's a great opportunity for him to establish himself as the authority in that niche. Another agent focuses on the equestrian niche, which helps her with selling farms and acreage properties. An agent out of Florida is doing well in a tough economy with her niche focusing on the "nudist" lifestyle. As odd as that might be for most agents, she has established trust and credibility with a sub culture of people who live this lifestyle. Focus on local restaurant reviews, school news, local sports leagues, local parks, ideas for family outings, or announce community events. The key is to be fresh, relevant, and relatable.

UNDERSTANDING SEARCH ENGINE TRAFFIC

Online niche brand marketing inherently increases highly targeted traffic by leveraging your niche content and SEO (Search Engine Optimization). SEO is a set of best practices and methods to improve where your website ranks in various keyword search results. Although the details of SEO are beyond the scope of this guide, the concepts are simple enough. Search engines crawl (or scan) pages on websites and index (or store) the content to be referenced later. This indexed content is then matched against the keywords used when a person is searching on sites like Google, AOL, Yahoo, or BING. Search engines determine which sites are most relevant for those search keywords and list results accordingly. For example, people searching for information on real estate communities or homes for sale will use specific search keywords to find relevant niche websites providing this information.

Imagine you are an agent in Georgia with a niche specializing in active adult living communities near Lake Lanier. Your website not only provides a list of homes for sale, but, also provides information on local restaurants and upcoming events for senior citizens. You post photo galleries and personal experiences of such events and write about the best places to eat and visit. Basically, you are just writing what you already know and are passionate about in your community. These are things you share with your friends and existing clients while out showing homes.

By publishing this knowledge to your website, you further establish your relevance and credibility with your community, with search engines, and with clients you've yet to meet. Senior citizens or their family members searching with the keywords, "Lake Lanier active adult living," will most likely come across your website and ultimately you.

BUILDING THE FOUNDATION FOR SUCCESS

You've just begun exploring the many concepts and principles of online niche brand marketing. However, the core principles discussed here will allow you to continue learning, implementing, and refining your marketing strategy. Remember to engage online as you would in person and not allow yourself to get lost in the technology. Focus on establishing credibility with niche content that authentically reflects your personality and experience. This niche content is the key to improving your search engine traffic and ultimately connecting you to more qualified clients. As long as you stay true to these principles, develop your niche content, you have the foundation necessary to overcome any technology issues, and ultimately, for achieving success.

About David

David Carroll established himself as an innovator in real estate technology after launching softRealty.com in 2007. Prior to entering the real estate industry, he acquired over a decade of experience architecting enterprise solutions for dozens of Fortune 500 companies, as well as, designing software for several technology startups. David has always had an inherent desire to help others leverage technology to make their lives easier and succeed in business. It was fate when he discovered the complex world of Multiple Listing Services (MLS) and the opportunity to help real estate agents use the Internet to connect with buyers outside their immediate circle of influence.

softRealty.com started as a Free MLS Property Search service for real estate agents to incorporate onto their websites. However, he quickly learned Free MLS Property Search wasn't enough. He then challenged the status quo with developing a new lead generation technology known as Anonymous Lead Capture. Anonymous Lead Capture gave real estate agents the opportunity to connect with anonymous website visitors actively searching for properties on their website. Utilizing analytics and a proprietary "In Network" messaging system, agents were able to capture, qualify, and engage with active buyers on their website.

David has been a speaker at prominent real estate technology conferences such as Inman Connect, RETechSouth, and Real Estate Bar Camps. Having engaged with heads of MLSs, National Brokerages, and real estate agents of influence these past few years, he has learned quite a bit about how real estate agents can thrive with technology and social media, even during the worst housing market of our time.

In late 2011, David incorporated this vast knowledge of how real estate agents should connect and market online with his extensive background in technology and launched WebSocial.ly – an online marketing platform for building socially optimized websites. WebSocial.ly takes the best practices of social media, search engine optimizations, and website design to help real estate agents and other professionals establish and dominate in their niche brand marketing.

About Gary

<u>EDUCATION</u>:

1986: Emory University, Atlanta, Georgia; B.A. degree in Political Science, and a minor in Afro-American and African Studies.

1989: J.D. from the Walter F. George School of Law of Mercer University, Macon, Georgia; Asst. Research Editor, Law Review; Vice President of the Student Bar Association, recipient of the Class of 1977 Scholarship Award.

Upon his graduation in 1989, Gary Martin Hays began his career in the insurance defense arena with the law firm BOVIS, KYLE & BURCH. In 1993, he and Duncan Maysilles formed the firm HAYS & MAYSILLES, P.C. in Atlanta. Upon Mr. Maysilles' retirement at the end of 1999, the firm has continued as the Law Offices of Gary Martin Hays & Associates, P.C. His firm specializes in personal injury, wrongful death, workers' compensation, and pharmaceutical claims.

His legal accomplishments include being a member of the prestigious Million Dollar Advocate's Forum, a society limited to those attorneys who have received a settlement or verdict of at least $1 Million Dollars. He has been recognized as a Super Lawyer in *Atlanta Magazine* as one of Georgia's top workers' compensation lawyers, as well as being selected as one of the Top 100 Trial Lawyers in Georgia since 2007 by the American Trial Lawyers Association. His law firm has recovered over $225 million, averaging about $20 million a year.

Gary Martin Hays is also a nationally-recognized safety advocate who works tirelessly to educate our families on issues ranging from bullying to Internet safety to abduction prevention. He serves on the Board of Directors of the **Elizabeth Smart Foundation** and has made numerous media appearances with Ed Smart on child safety initiatives. He has appeared on countless television stations, including the ABC, CBS, NBC and FOX affiliates. He has been interviewed on over 110 radio stations, including the Georgia News Network. He currently hosts *"Georgia Behind The Scenes"* on the CW Atlanta TV Network. He has been featured in *USA Today, The Wall Street Journal,* and over 250 online sites including Morningstar.com, CBS News's MoneyWatch.com, the *Boston Globe, The Miami Herald, The New York Daily News*, and The Miami Herald. He is a co-author of the book *"Trendsetters"* which was a best-seller in two categories on Amazon.com in 2011.

In 2008, Gary started the non-profit organization **Keep Georgia Safe.org** with the mission to provide safety education and crime prevention training in Georgia. Keep Georgia Safe has trained over 80 state and local law enforcement officers in CART (Child Abduction Response Teams) so our first responders will know what to do in the event a child is abducted in Georgia. Gary has completed Child Abduction Response Team training with the National AMBER Alert program through the U.S. Department of Justice and Fox Valley Technical College. In 2007, he was awarded Georgia Trial Lawyer's Community Service Award for his charitable endeavors for the American Cancer Society, the Leukemia & Lymphoma Society, St. Jude's Children's Research Hospital, and Dream House for Medically Fragile Children. His law firm has given away 1,000 bicycle helmets and 14 college scholarships.

CHAPTER 9

7 Title Insurance Tips and Secrets
These could save you hundreds of dollars at your next closing

By Kevin Tacher

INTRODUCTION TO TITLE INSURANCE

Before we get into the details of the *7* *Title Insurance Tips and Secrets* to help you save hundreds of dollars at your next closing, I would like to introduce you to the history of Title Insurance.

Title Insurance is issued in the United States upon the purchase of real property. A title insurance policy ensures that you have clear and marketable title to a property when you close. Title insurance has many facets to it, like lien searches, title commitments, title policies, etc. Wikipedia defines title insurance as "indemnity insurance against financial loss from defects in title to real property and from the invalidity or unenforceability of mortgage liens."

Title Insurance is unique to the United States and is not offered in many other countries. The need for title insurance came about due to the deficiency of the United States land record laws, which did not protect a purchaser of real property from title defects in the past. The purpose of title insurance is to protect a buyer of a property and ensure that prior to purchasing, all outstanding liens, judgments, etc. that are attached to that property are satisfied or resolved. Once resolved, the title will be considered clear and marketable, meaning the property can be sold. The title company then issues a title policy which specifically outlines the amount of title insurance the policy covers (usually the purchase price or the amount of the loan recorded against the property). It is possible to buy real estate without a title policy, but to do so would be extremely foolish, since it would expose the buyer to any problems that occurred with that property prior to them purchasing it.

Title insurance protects the owner of the property as well as the lender's financial interest in the property against loss – due to defects in title, liens, judgments, etc. A lien that shows up in a title search will cause the title to be clouded (defective) and will make the title unmarketable. What this means is that unless the buyer is willing to buy the property with the existing defect, the property cannot be transferred prior to the defect being resolved.

Title insurance also will defend against a lawsuit attacking the title, because the title policy covers the insured and will reimburse the insured for the actual monetary loss incurred, up to the dollar amount of insurance provided by the policy. It is important to remember that title insurance protects the owner and/or lender from defects that arose prior to the date of purchase. It is not like traditional insurance that protects future risk.

DO I NEED TITLE INSURANCE?

When you are wondering if you should incur the extra cost of having the owner's portion of a title insurance policy, what do you tell yourself? Do you think to yourself... *"Is the extra cost worth it?"*

The best answer is always, "Yes, it's worth it." The last thing you would want to have happen is for you to incur a cost, or to lose a home, because you had skipped the owner's title insurance.

What can happen? There are a whole variety of obscure issues that can affect the validity of your title.

For example, an IRS lien that was imposed on one spouse in the days when the IRS did not extend a collection action to the other spouse could now impact on your title.

Or a family member of the seller has an unrecorded interest in the title that pops up after you complete your closing.

If you get a loan, you must pay for the lender's portion of title insurance – it's worth the extra premium payment to also include the owner's portion. You will sleep better knowing that you are protected against any future claim.

SHOULD I USE MY TITLE COMPANY OR THE BANKS TITLE COMPANY?

In Florida, it is customary for the seller to pay for the title policy and to pick the title agent. The exceptions are Broward and Miami-Dade Counties where it is customary for the buyer to pay for the title policy and to pick the title agent. Usually, whoever picks the title agent also pays for the title insurance policy.

If you are buying bank-owned properties then you should be especially cautious. If you are using the bank's title company then this means that the title company has a relationship with the seller and not with you. There have been several cases where our investors have used the banks title company and had serious title defects.

The title companies that represent the bank are typically known as "title mills" which means that they are closing hundreds or thousands of transactions per month. This means that the bank is effectively the title company's biggest and best client, and so the title company is much more concerned with the relationship with the bank than with you. Another issue is that because they are processing so many files, they make many mistakes, which your title company that represents you, may not make.

One example of an issue that we have seen is where there was an open code enforcement violation against a property that was going to cost a buyer over $5,000 to remedy. It was the bank's title company's procedure to have the buyer sign a hold harmless agreement, which effectively means that the banks title company is willing to close the transaction with a title defect and make it the buyer's problem. This is a classic example of why you don't want to let the bank choose the title company, even if it saves you money. You are better off paying for your own title policy and choosing your own title company that will have your best interests at heart.

Another issue if you plan on simultaneous or double closing a transaction with the banks title company, will be that they will simply disallow you from going through with the second closing. Many title companies that represent the banks are unfamiliar with these types of closings and how the procedure works. If you are planning on a simultaneous or double closing on the property with an end buyer, then using the banks title company could effectively prevent your transaction from closing – which would eliminate your profit. This is yet another reason why you want to choose your title company.

Lastly, if you plan on closing an REO transaction, time is of the essence. It is important for the title company to record the deed as soon as possible. This becomes an issue when you are planning to resell to an FHA buyer and there are seasoning requirements. We have seen several cases where the bank's title company holds on to a batch of deeds and waits as long as thirty days to record these deeds.

If you have a relationship with a title company, they should use a courier to immediately deliver the document to the courthouse for recording. If you are simultaneous or double closing, then it is imperative that the deeds are recorded in the correct sequence – preventing a chain of title defect. This is yet another example of why you should always choose your own title company.

7 TITLE INSURANCE TIPS AND SECRETS

Secret #1 - Simultaneous Policies

If you buy a house and get an owner's title policy for $100,000 and obtain financing to buy the house, the lender will require their own title insurance policy. This policy is called a simultaneous policy – which means that you pay full price for the owner's policy and you get the simultaneous policy for a promulgated rate of only $25. Many title companies increase the cost from $25 to $250 or more. Knowing this tip can save you hundreds of dollars at every closing.

Secret #2 - Promulgated Rate

Title insurance promulgated rates are the lowest title insurance premiums a title company is allowed to charge. That is, the state sets a minimum rate and title companies have to charge a rate that is the same or higher than this promulgated rate. It would benefit you to know what the states promulgated rate is in order to see how much you are being charged over the minimum rate. Know what the promulgated rate is in your state and don't pay more than this minimum rate. As a title company, we believe that charging more than this rate is not justified for our clients. Unfortunately not all settlement agents feel the same way. Closing costs vary substantially. That is why the new RESPA laws were established in order to make the market more competitive and fair for the consumer.

Secret #3 – Escrow Agreements and Deposits

You should always use an escrow agreement. This stipulates, in the event of a default by one party, what the procedure and instructions are for the title company or attorney, and how they should manage the escrow dispute and release of the escrow deposit.

When you receive proof of deposit for your buyers, you want to make sure that the title company has received and cleared good funds into their escrow account. For this reason, you should make sure that all deposits are in cleared funds only. Try not to accept personal checks if you do not know the buyer and if their funds will clear. A stop payment can be issued on cashier's checks or printed fraudulently. Its best practice to insist on a wire transfer in order to ensure that the deposits are cleared funds. The same applies to the funds required for closing. Always use wire transfers if you want to be safe.

Secret #4 - Reissue Rate Credit

If the seller can produce a policy that was issued in the past three years to the title company, then the title company can provide a reissue rate that can be a substantial savings. Always ask the seller if they have a copy of their original title insurance policy if they purchased the property in the previous three years. You can receive this reissue rate credit for your new owners' title policy. The actual amount of the credit is the same amount regardless of whether the policy is one, two or three years old. If the policy is older than three years then you will not be able to receive the reissue credit.

In the case of a refinance, you can get a reissue credit if you can provide a copy of your owners' title policy regardless of when you purchased the property. It is imperative that you store your title policy in a safe and secure place such as a safe.

Secret #5 – Can you prepare your own Deed

A common issue that we see when it comes to title examination is the use of deeds that are purchased at the local store. While these deeds are valid and can be used, you need to keep a few things in mind. When you first purchase a property, you are taking legal title. Why would you jeopardize your equitable interest in the property by preparing a fill in the blank document from the local store? There are many title companies and attorneys that would prepare a deed for minimal expense. This is especially true if you have an existing relationship with them. Should you decide to prepare one of these deeds yourself, please keep a few items in mind. In Florida, all deeds should include the name of the grantor (seller) and grantee (buyer). Deeds should include the marital status of all parties. The complete legal description and parcel identification number should be included. Please do not copy the legal description from the county property appraiser's office website as this is usually an abbreviated version. Finally, make sure the deed contains a signature of the grantor (seller), two witnesses and a notary.

Secret #6 – Controlled Business Arrangements

A Controlled Business Arrangement is where a bank, real estate agent, mortgage broker, or title company may have an agreement with each other to provide their services to their clients for a referral fee in return. While this is not illegal or necessarily unethical, you always want to ask the question "Do you have a controlled business arrangement with anyone involved in this transaction?" This is especially important with real estate because you want to make sure that your best interest is being protected. Unfortunately, some individuals are more concerned about getting their referral fee as opposed to representing their client's best interests. Please note that it is a violation of Florida Bar regulations for an attorney to pay a referral fee to any person other than another attorney.

Secret #7 – Do you Interview your Title Company?

Do you interview your Title Company before you choose them to close? If not, then try and ask these questions the next time you have a closing.

- Ask them if they are experts in their field, or if they are a "middleman" company that refers their business out to another firm to issue your policy.

- Take a look at the company's name or website for a clue if they are a real company. There is so much fraud you want to make sure you are dealing with a reputable company.

- Do they have a database of satisfied, well-known customers, or just a list of anonymous "testimonials" that could have been written by anyone? Ask them to supply you with verifiable references. If they can't, chances are they don't want you to find out something you shouldn't. I would suggest calling at least two of their customers to verify the company's integrity.

- Will they actually follow through on your transaction, or just skip town leaving you to start at the beginning? Are they ethical and do they implement world class business practices? Do they have an actual phone number that dials through to a live person or a virtual assistant?

I hope you enjoyed reading the *7* Title Insurance Tips and Secrets as much as I enjoyed sharing them with you. If you can remember a few things from this chapter, please remember the following:

- Always get a title insurance policy for all transactions.
- Always choose your own title company to represent you.
- Always review the title commitment prior to closing.
- Always ask questions if you do not understand something.
- Do not sign your closing documents until you have reviewed them for accuracy.

If you enjoyed reading this chapter, I would like to offer you a free download of my entire book, Title Insurance Tips and Secrets. Please visit: www.TitleRate.com

I hope that you choose Independence Title for your next closing. However, if you don't, I hope that you learned something useful from this chapter. Finally, remember to watch out for potential problems at your next closing.

I wish you great success as a real estate investor, real estate professional or consumer.

About Kevin

Kevin Tacher - also known as *"The Title King"* - is the founder and Chief Executive Officer of Independence Title, Inc. a Fort Lauderdale, Florida based title insurance company. Kevin is a *Published Author and National Speaker.* Kevin has shared the stage with some of the country's best real estate and motivational speakers. As a trailblazer in the industry, Kevin founded the **nationally-recognized website TitleRate. com,** which is the leading source for title insurance rates, real estate mobile applications, and up to date real estate information and education. Kevin values community relationships and is involved with LifeNet4Families, formally known as the Cooperative Feeding Program of Broward County, whose purpose is to reduce the pain and suffering of individuals and families in poverty. He was appointed to the Board of Directors in 2010.

Prior to moving to Florida in 2001, Kevin grew up in Long Island, NY and was firefighter and Fire Safety Director for the Crowne Plaza Hotel in New York City. He moved to Florida only twenty days before September 11th. Professionally, Kevin has worked and held licenses as a mortgage consultant, real estate broker, and title insurance agent. Armed with extensive knowledge and experience in the real estate industry, Kevin opened Independence Title. Kevin's previous real estate experience enables him to provide a complete range of knowledge for homeowners and real estate professionals throughout the State of Florida. Kevin's enjoys scuba diving, fishing, and lives in South Florida with his daughter, Lindsay Rose.

You can read more of Kevin's material on his blog at: www.TitleRate.com

To learn more about Kevin Tacher, "The Title King" and how you can receive a full downloadable copy of his book, **Title Insurance Tips and Secrets,** please visit: www.TitleRate.com or call 954-335-9305.

Referral… *I've worked with Kevin for several years and he has proven many times to be a person of integrity that possesses great knowledge in his industry. Kevin never fails to offer praise and recommendations for his associates and business partners. Kevin is constantly striving to improve his business and seeking ways to help others. I fully recommend him in every way for all Florida Real Estate Closings. – David Dweck, Founder of the Boca Real Estate Investment Club*

CHAPTER 10

The Boring Basics

By Rick Geha

Prospecting, Lead Generating, Cold-Calling, Door Knocking, Open Houses, Internet Lead Generation, Recruiting, Inviting, Presenting, Floor Time, Up Desk, Agent On Call...(Please, if you've come up with other, more imaginative names for Lead Generation, let me know!)

After more than 31 years of selling homes in Northern California, I'm so excited to write about this entertaining, and yet sometimes depressing subject. After all, I've spent years creating every reason possible to avoid Lead Generation. That being said, that was the equivalent of me spending years avoiding ways to make a ton more money than I was making. In fact, I have actual proof that it works when you do it.... (Imagine that!!)

There are maybe (and I'm exaggerating) 9 people in the whole world who throw the blankets off, first thing in the morning, and yell out loud... "I'm SO excited to **PROSPECT** today!!"... Really... who does that?? Not me... not many.... there are those few, the disciplined, the focused, the decided, the committed... they get to it, every day, same time, same place...and they get **RESULTS!**

I think it's safe to say that you know that "Lead Generation" defined, is ... whatever actions it takes YOU to get leads that will now, or one day, buy or sell through you. That's it! No magic. Please don't get caught up in wordy or lofty definitions of Lead Generation, or rules about what constitutes Lead Generation. Don't get bogged down with deciding if what you're doing is passive lead generation versus active lead generation. WHY?? Because if you will just spend productive time getting and measuring your results, you can avoid all of the judgment about how you're getting those results. …Especially from your harshest critic.

YOU!

I'm shortening a very long story. I began my real estate career on May 5, 1980. I was 22. I was still in college, working at a restaurant, and squeezing real estate in between everything else. My broker was my Uncle Bill. He had already been in the business for 17 years. My ONLY training was like this: "There's a desk with a phone. There's a reverse phone directory in the drawer. Now get to work!"

My earliest memories include AVOIDING anything that seemed uncomfortable in the way of generating leads. I knocked on doors. I made 'cold' calls. I was rejected often. It hurt! I usually could only tolerate it for 15 minutes, before I found an excuse to stop. I remember putting an ad in the paper and it worked! I got some calls and was able to sell a house or two because of the ad. As I look back, that ad pushed me to find more ways to avoid prospecting, and to avoid any direct encounters. Financially, this wasn't working.

As I learned to ask questions, and make my own way, I discovered Mike Ferry, Howard Brinton, Walter Sanford, Allan Domb, Ralph Rogers, Steve Westmark, Mary Harker, and in the years after 1991, many others who were creating HUGE incomes and were willing to teach, coach, mentor and share, so that I, too, could find my way. They, collectively, became my new heroes. I listened to everything they said and did. I knew I didn't want to spend money anymore, so I did everything I could not to. I stopped hiding behind mailers and ads and started looking for ways to get face-to-face, or phone-to- phone, with as many people as possible.

I had essentially, without knowing, decided that I wanted to build a prospecting-based business where about 70% of my business would continue to be referral and repeat, and 30% would be 'new' business, meaning business that came from my different methods of lead generating. *Simply put, I got comfortable being uncomfortable!* Rejection and what people 'may' have thought of me was no longer bothering me! So…enough about my failures. Let's outline what exactly are… "The Boring Basics."

1. Build Solid, Long Lasting Relationships. Some trainers will tell you that this business is a 'numbers' business. Other trainers will tell you that this business is a 'relationships' business. I believe it to be a "Numbers OF Relationships" Business. *In life, AND in real estate, he/she with the most NUMBER of solid, long-lasting, and symbiotic relationships, WINS EVERYTIME.* If you are always seeking relationships so that YOU can make more money, or that they will buy or sell from you, hang it up now! People can detect hidden agendas. These types of relationships are built from being INTERESTED, not INTERESTING. Learn to be a great listener! Turn OFF your inner brain, and zip your lip. Let them see that this relationship you're building with them is built on 'unconditional' giving. What YOU can do for them has to be at the forefront of your thoughts, always. Remember, too, that behaviorally, we are all not the same. Naturally, some are better listeners, some like to talk more, some don't like people all that much, and some want to over think things. Allow your intelligence to guide you into a behavior that will best serve you when it comes to building relationships.

   A. Mail to your KNOWN Database (people you know, either a little, or very well!) at least once per month. I prefer real mail, in the mailbox. Some of you refer to that as 'snail mail.' It works. You know your KNOWN Database better than I do, so if you think they'll feel 'touched' when you send them email, by all means, send them email. I am not a proponent of spending money for no reason at all. When you can afford to, if it's snail mail, or immediately if it's email, send them something twice per month. Something that has perceived value to THEM! They don't want to hear boring stories about you, unless there is perceived value in the moral of the story.

B. Call your KNOWN Database at least 3 times per year. "What do I say???" Just call them. The first time you call, say… "I'm just calling to apologize." They'll ask you why you are apologizing. You'll say… "Because it's been so long since we've talked. Totally my fault. I'm finding out that I have lost touch with you, and many other friends like you, as a result of not picking up the phone. I'm never letting that happen again." They'll say something like… no worries, it's okay.…. and you'll say,.…. "No, ..it's not okay. Tell you what… I'm so committed to staying in touch, that if you'll give me your birthday, I'll send you something every year on your birthday!" They'll say,.…. "you will??"… You say…. "Yes. And give me your husband's birthday, too… and, while I have you, what's your wedding anniversary?" Now you have reasons to be in touch with them. Put all of this information in a reliable contact management system. Keep your notes up to date. Send them something small, yet meaningful on their birthdays. Here in CA, we send them a $1 Lotto Scratcher in a handwritten card. They LOVE it! DO NOT ask for business on the apology call. On ALL of the calls after that first apology call….ASK FOR BUSINESS! They won't mind…they like you.. You know that because it's your KNOWN Database… PEOPLE YOU KNOW!

C. Whether you reach them or not on your calls, send them a hand-written note after each call. Say something in the note that refers to your conversation when you spoke to them, or, if you left them a voice mail, say that in the card.

D. Earlier, you got 'her birthday', 'his birthday', and their 'wedding anniversary' on your apology call. Make sure that on these dates, they get a card AND a call!! Lots to do, AND…worth it…

E. Make sure that A, B, C, and D above exceed 30 'touches' per year. This way, you will never be forgotten. Follow up often! Remember that the ONLY thing that can replace the importance of a phone call, is seeing them, or visiting them in person.

2. ASK FOR REFERRALS OFTEN. Unfortunately, most of us don't ask for referrals, ever! Some of us ask for referrals AFTER the deal is done. Quite frankly, the best time to ask for referrals is RIGHT NOW! No joke…. If you do everything that I said in #1 above, and that you truly have EVERYONE'S best interests in mind, always, NO ONE will mind giving you referrals. Whether you are new, experienced, or just contemplating the business, understand from now, that if you are currently 'working with a prospect,' it is not too soon to ask for a referral. The most oft overlooked part of referrals is getting referrals from other agents. This, too, is just a matter of relationships. Don't go to meetings and conventions and pass out hundreds of cards! Don't go and only sit and mingle with those you already know from your office or your home market! Any possible chance you have from this day forward, spend quality time with Realtors who do business everywhere but where you do business. Brainstorm, mastermind, and stay in touch. Again, wherever you are and there are Realtors, create relationships and ask for referrals.

NOTE**** Repeat and Referral Business will come, in abundance, from what you will do above in #1 and #2. An ideal real estate sales business, as I mentioned earlier, will involve about 67 to 70 % repeat and referral business and about 30 to 33% of new business. It is the best of all worlds if those percentages stay the same, while the number of closed units goes up. I hear agents often say that there business is 95% referral and they are so proud of that. Frankly, there's no reason not to be proud of that. What if, though, your NUMBER of referrals went up, and the percentage of referrals as part of your business went down? In other words, you had more referrals next year AND you got some NEW BUSINESS that came from prospecting, the Internet or Social Media or something. Let's say it was 10 more transactions because you actually Lead Generated. Now you have 10 more names in your KNOWN Database that will be able to refer you! It's a HUGE win for you.

3. NEW BUSINESS: This is a very broad-based subject that spans the entire world of the Internet all the way to the very simplest 'cold call'. Simply put, NEW business would represent anything that wasn't a repeat client or a referral.

A. WEB: PRESENCE, SITES, SOCIAL MEDIA. Craigslist, Postlets.com, Trulia, Zillow, Google, and many more sites are available where you can create presence and ads that combine FREE and, either PPC (Pay Per Click) or SEO (Search Engine Optimization). I have facilitated many panels involving those who specialize in using websites, the Internet, and, of course, Social Media to improve upon their current business, and to take it to an entirely new level. "Social Media 101" and "The 33 Million People In The Room" are two books that are great on this subject. Seek Wisdom! Really make a concerted effort to ask those who are doing well in this area to share with you! I'm a Baby Boomer, so don't look to me!

B. OPEN HOUSES: Make them an 'event', not a task! Plan ahead! Door knock at least 100 doors before every open house. Plan a 'sneak preview' ONLY for neighbors and let them know. Have at least 10 signs. While it's costly, if you can use as many as 35 signs, (assuming that's legal where you live) you will see results that will astound you. Advertise all over your MLS and the Web, or wherever it's free.

C. FSBO's and EXPIRED's: For Sale By Owners and Expired Listings are always abundant, and, incredible ways to get more listings. Again,.. SEEK WISDOM… ask around and see who is doing it well, and, take them to lunch. There are many 'systems' out there that you can buy, and some of them are very cheap. If you want to jump in without training…just remember…build a relationship, and ask them how you can be of service.

D. COLD CALLING and DOOR KNOCKING….What can I say? If you have never done these two types of prospecting, you haven't lived! It's truly a rush the first time you get business from these. Much easier than you have heard, and…. A lot less painful than described by others not in the know. This is truly best done by "just freakin' do it!" "What have you heard about the real estate market in our area?" is a good question to ask. "The Real Estate Market is UNBELIEVABLE!" is a great thing to say during your conversations. When they ask "why?"… Remind them about lower prices, more inventory, lowest interest rates in 50 years, just to name a few… Get out there today!

E. FARMING: Demographic and Geographic. Demographic is 'dripping' on a 'category', if you will, Iike: Financial Planners, Divorce Attorneys, Your Bike Club, Your Bowling Club, Your Church Roster (if allowed), Age groups, Surnames, or anything else that strikes you as Lead worthy. Geographic is typically homes in clusters or contiguous. You want to get these to big numbers as soon as you can afford to. You can door knock and call for these, also. If you want to do several thousand, which becomes very lucrative after year 3, you'll want to stick to mailing. Remember,.. to make this category work, to get real results, you'll want to hit them with a mailer every month ONCE (at the very least and most recommended). If you cannot do ONCE per month, EVERY month for at least 3 years, financially, then DON'T START! Really! The stats show that you will get your biggest return after 30 months! You can expect (rough numbers) about 1 deal per year, for every 100 homes or names you are farming per month. (i.e., if you're farming 2000 homes per month, by year 3 you could be getting 20 deals per year from that farm). Consistency here wins every time!

My gosh! Where has the time gone? It's time for me to run, so let me leave you with some parting thoughts. There are MANY other ways to create leads. Radio shows, television shows, marketing through print media, and so on. What I have listed here are not only the most 'basic,' they are the most lucrative. They create the most results, in the least amount of time – especially if you're considering quality of the leads and the ones most convertible into appointments. So, it's likely that this chapter has just been a brief recap of things you've heard, or, things you already know. I have learned more about this subject in the past 7 years, than my first 24 years in real estate combined! I am a student of Lead Gen, and I want you to become the same! Make "Seek Wisdom" your daily mantra!

Lead Generation truly is the one thing that EVERYONE knows that we MUST do, and, at the same time EVERYONE finds ways to NOT DO! WHY? As I've said, it's the pain of being uncomfortable. Believe me… the pain of no income is worse, by a lot. A long time friend of mine and author and speaker, Dave Jenks, once said: "Lead Generation is the most important thing to do, every single day! And, when you have time for nothing else, it's the ONLY thing you do!"

About Rick

Rick Geha began his real estate career at 22 years old, on May 5, 1980. He immediately began part-time sales at his Uncle's small independent in Fremont, California. He was working in his mom's restaurant and at Fed Ex, along with selling real estate part time.

In 1987, he went full time, quitting everything else, as he was selling more part-time than everyone else in his office was selling full time. By 1989, he was in the top 1% of the Southern Alameda County Board of Realtors.

In 1993, he left the family-owned business and went to work for a small office of 20 agents, one of 21 offices of a large independent. He was a 'Selling Manager.' He grew that office, which eventually became a CENTURY 21, to over 100 agents, while still being one of the top 10 producers in Fremont. That CENTURY 21 Office, was recognized as NUMBER 2 in VOLUME CLOSED, WORLDWIDE for CENTURY 21 in 1999 and 2000, and was #6 in UNITS CLOSED. In 2001, that office was changed to a Coldwell Banker, and he set out to look for a new home.

Loving the CULTURE and the Training and Education supplied by the company, Rick fell in love with, and joined Keller Williams Realty. That was November of 2001. Today, a little over 9 years later, he is part owner of 6 Keller Williams Realty Franchises in Northern California, and is the Operating Principal of 4 of them. He still sells as part of the Rick Geha Real Estate Team, mostly playing the role of the Lead Generator. His Team closed about $29 Million in '09 and $27 Million in '10.

It was at Keller Williams he discovered his passion for speaking, training and facilitating. He regularly emcees 7 to 10 non-profit events per year, and now does almost 100 (1-day) seminars around the US and Canada for Keller Williams, along with KEYNOTE speeches for companies and corporations of all kinds, and has recently completed his first motivational and inspirational CD. He brings over 30 years of real estate experience and passion to his speaking.

CHAPTER 11

Seller-Financed Real Estate
The New Profit Paradigm

By Jason Watson

We all remember the days of easy credit and rapid-fire home sales – just a few years ago, real estate was an amazing business to be in, right?

Then suddenly, it wasn't so great. And then the Wall Street meltdown hit. And *then* credit was no longer so easy and home sales were a lot harder to make.

This is all, of course, recent history that I don't really need to repeat to anyone reading this book. If you're in real estate, you all know where you were then – and where you are now.

But I'd like to tell you about where I was then, …and where I am now. I changed up my entire approach to buying and selling homes - with a system of seller-financed real estate transactions - that provide me with a continuous cash flow and substantial ongoing profits.

MAKING THE TRANSITION

I began my real estate career as a licensed realtor in the Calgary,

Alberta area in 1999 – and achieved a great deal of success. At my peak, I owned three real estate offices that had over 200 real estate agents working out of them. But, to tell you the truth, I was already beginning to become bored with the conventional methods of selling homes and investing in real estate – which is why I ended up selling those offices in 2007.

When the recession hit and banks began tightening credit, I knew the real estate landscape was in for a long-term change. I began to look for different routes to expedite home sales – because the majority of the population now couldn't obtain the financing to close a real estate deal.

A large reason for that in my area, …in the province of Alberta, the banks removed the ability of home buyers to assume the existing mortgages of the sellers without any qualifications. Suddenly, a home buyer's only resort was to obtain his or her own mortgage – at a time when the banks were making that task more difficult than ever.

That's when I decided to explore seller-financed real estate deals. I had already been aware of their existence, but I had never really seriously considered this alternative. Prior to the recession, it never seemed necessary, but my business mentor reawakened me to the concept – and I saw where, in this new economic climate, it just might be a way to realize more profits in a tight financial time.

I had bought and sold real estate as an investor while I was a licensed realtor, but only on the side, not as a full-time endeavor. Now, I began to look at using the seller-financed option to sell some of that investment property in the most profitable way possible. I didn't re-invent the wheel with the systems I created, but I did take the information that was out there and fine-tuned it to make it work as well as possible.

Basically, how it works is that you become the bank. You control the assets so you are able to make the rules. You basically take the bank mortgage debt you have on the property (assuming you have a mortgage), and wrap it with your new mortgage that you create personally with an interest rate that's 25 to 50% (or more if your market can handle it) over the bank mortgage you have. You can also increase the value of the home to increase your profits, as well as charge your own lending fees, just as happens in a private mortgage transaction.

CRUNCHING THE NUMBERS

To really understand how a seller-financed real estate deal works, let's break down a typical deal in terms of how the numbers can work with a home that's valued at $350,000.

Let's say I own that home. If I sold it the normal way through a realtor on the MLS in the market I work in, I'd probably make the sale for about $340,000. Take away about $25,000 in real estate fees, mortgage payout penalties and closing costs, I would be left with about $315,000. And again, in today's credit climate, it could be difficult to find a qualified buyer.

By going the seller-financed route, however, this financial picture changes dramatically.

Let's now say I already have a $290,000 mortgage in place with a bank that's at a 3% interest rate – with payments around $1220.00 a month. To begin with, utilizing a seller-financed deal and making it easy to buy, I can increase the price of the house 5 to 10% to say $370,000 (as a side note, don't add too much value to a home – otherwise, your buyer will have difficulty financing a new mortgage down the road to buy you out).

I'm also going to ask the potential buyer for around a 5%-plus down payment – for this example, let's use a figure of $20,000. They pay the $20,000 and they now must take a mortgage from me for around $350,000. And since I am doing this mortgage personally, I'm going to charge an interest rate of 5.25% (2.25% higher than the mortgage I have with the bank on the same property). Their mortgage payments end up at around $1932.00 a month, over $700 more than I have to put up for my monthly mortgage payment with the bank.

So let's review where we are so far. I've received a $20,000 down payment that actually, for all intents and purposes, is found money since I upped the value of the house for the sale. My mortgage with the buyer ($350,000) is also worth $60,000 more than the mortgage I have with the bank ($290,000). So I'm already up $55,000 (difference between $315,000 and $350,000 + $20,000 down payment) and, since I'm charging 2.25% more interest on a higher mortgage with the buyer, that amount really begins to skyrocket.

And we're not done yet. I'm also going to charge the buyer the traditional lending fee (or loan origination fee) of around 3%, or roughly another $10,500. That takes the mortgage up to $360,500.00 ($370,000.00 - $20,000.00 = $350,000.00 +3%) And finally I've also added in a 2% (or the interest differential) repayment fee, similar to what happens at the closing of a traditional mortgage closing.

As you can see, the profits can be incredible from this kind of seller-financed home sale. Before calculating the cash flow and my bank mortgage reduction I receive an additional $65,000.00!

MAKING YOUR SELLER-FINANCED DEAL

Now, obviously, since you are taking on a big obligation here by personally placing a mortgage with the buyer, you need to be careful about several aspects of these deals. I'd like to review some of these points at this time.

- **Line Up Your Mortgages**
  Your existing mortgage with the bank should come due no earlier than 90 days before the due date of the buyer's mortgage with you. That's because if the bank's mortgage is due and they don't want to extend or renew it, you want to make sure you can pay them in full. This gives you a 90 day period to work with the buyers to pay off their mortgage to you.

- **Get Enough Down**

  I would not do one of these deals with anything less than a 5% down payment of the purchase price from the home buyer. I'm most comfortable with at least 10% down – but, on the other hand, the less the buyer puts down, the higher you can charge on fees and rates – since your risk is going up. For anything less than 15% down, you also need to make sure the buyer is going to live in the home and not treat it as a rental. Generally, a primary residence mortgage will be paid before other bills like a visa, L.O.C., or rental properties, if money is tight.

- **Get Independent Legal Advice**

  You should always double-check on what the lending and real estate laws are in the area you live in. And you should also have the home buyer pre-sign as many forms as possible that will help you avoid a lengthy foreclosure process should the buyer ultimately be unable to make the mortgage payments. In Alberta, for example, we have what's called a "Quit Claim" that I have my buyers sign in advance – it "helps" eliminates long, drawn-out issues if they can't pay down the road.

- **Keep It In Your Name**

  During the length of the buyer's mortgage with you, you want to keep the property deed or title in your name. That way, if the house becomes worth more than the actual mortgage, the buyer can't go out and borrow against the equity in the home and get into a possible bad debt situation – which could mean you end up having to work with another financial institution and foreclose on the home. You don't want that scenario.

  One exception to the rule is when the buyers have a large down payment and insists to have the title or deed in their names. To secure your position be sure to register your mortgage to the buyer against the title or deed. You may also want to register the loan amount for the full purchase price of the property to avoid having additional mortgages registered with your lender and again having to work with that lender, or worse yet, foreclose.

You also don't want to allow the buyer to transfer the title or deed to another party – put a clause in the documents that if they do attempt to transfer it, the mortgage is immediately due. Again, you want to keep control.

- **Check Out Your Potential Buyer**
  Before you follow through with a seller-financed deal, make sure the buyer can actually afford the payments. With these deals, it doesn't really matter if their credit isn't that wonderful, what's critical is their income (and also, the worse their credit is, the bigger your risk – which, again, means you can charge more on rates and fees). The monthly payment they're going to need to make (principle, interest, insurance, taxes, etc.) should never be higher than 50% of their monthly income. You should also require the buyer to personally guarantee the debt.

- **Preserve Your Credit**
  When you're wrapping the mortgage debt with your bank mortgage, you need to make sure all bills come through to you so they get paid in an expedient manner. For example, bills for insurance and property or land taxes should go directly to you. You can simply break down those bill amounts and add them to the buyer's monthly mortgage payments.

- **Protect Your Property**
  You should put in the mortgage documents that the buyer cannot do major alterations to the home without your written approval. Obviously, minor work like carpeting and painting isn't a problem, but the bigger things you want to control. You don't want them tearing apart the entire house to do a complete remodel job unless you agree to it.

- **Create a Safety Account**

  As much as people who are making mortgage payments towards ownership are more reliable than stereotypical "tenants" who are renting, there can still be financial problems down the road. Buyers can lose jobs or other income and suddenly have difficulty paying. You, however, want to make sure you can keep paying the bank mortgage - so always keep a minimum of three months worth of payments in an account for that purpose.

When you compare the numbers, seller-financed home sales are much more lucrative than conventional real estate deals, especially in today's difficult economy. Judge for yourself with the example of the $350,000 house. Sell it through the MLS and you realize only $315,000 of that $350,000. Do a seller-financed deal, you receive the spread over your mortgage with the bank, you receive the down payment that's basically just extra value you've added on to your home, and you also receive the hefty fees and points that come with being a mortgage lender, as well as the mortgage reduction with the bank mortgage from the monthly payments. That's a lot more than you could ever imagine getting from a conventional deal.

I have people paying off mortgages they have with me at this moment – and my cash flow is excellent because of it. Seller-financing also enables home sales that wouldn't ordinarily happen - meaning you wouldn't be making any money at all if this system wasn't in play. I also believe seller-financing will become even more popular, considering the recent U.S. credit downgrade and banks putting even tighter lending restrictions in place.

If you own a property and are interested in getting into the seller-financed game, you have several options. If you put the sale together yourself, where you finance your house and collect the payments from the buyer, or you can sell the transaction (the mortgage and property) to another investor. And you can make that sale either for face value, or discount it by $15 or $20,000 to increase the yield for a new investor. If you do the discount, you still end up with $50,500.00 if we use the $350,000 house template.

Of course, when you do sell to an investor, you must do your due diligence on the buyers you sold and financed the house to. The investor will want to verify that they can continue the seller-financed mortgage payments and successfully complete the transaction.

If you don't own property or are looking to increase your investment portfolio and are interested in getting into the seller-financed arena, there are several ways to do so. You can go out and buy a house, then turn around and do a seller-financed sale. You can be one of the investors I just discussed who buy one of these transactions after the deal is already in place. You can even take advantage of government grants in the country that help with these kinds of transactions.

If you'd like advice on doing your own seller-financed home sales, or are just interested in investing in one of these transactions, I invite you to contact me directly at jason@thewatsongroup.com. I will also share with you a few recommended App's and software to help you with the process.

There is still a way to make significant profits in the real estate business – and I firmly believe that seller-financing is a key to those profits.

About Jason

Jason Watson´s high-energy approach, superior negoti-ating skills and outstanding business sense are reasons why he was one of Calgary's top Realtors. His extensive knowledge and experience in the industry has enabled him to develop the skills and influence to excel in any Real Estate Market!

After being raised on a farm in Central Alberta, Jason really knows the value of a dollar. He grew up being responsible for raising his own calves to sell at auction. Learning the fundamentals of business at such an early age in-spired Jason to constantly pursue new challenges, hone his sales skills and develop his mind for business. As soon as Jason arrived in Calgary, he saw the huge potential for investment and profit in the Calgary housing market and knew his calling was in the real estate industry.

This one-time farm boy was a licensed REALTOR® from 1999-2009, and had been involved in over 700 residential and commercial sales transactions. He has received numerous awards throughout his career. Additionally, Jason is an avid real estate investor himself, and reaped the benefits of real estate investment first hand, fuelling his passion for the industry.

One of Jason´s past endeavours was establishing a real estate brokerage from the ground up. Buying out two real estate companies and merging with a third office, Jason grew his brokerage to accommodate over 190 REALTORS® in only 7.5 months. Jason went on to win a "Broker of the Year Award" and ulti-mately experienced great success. After 2 years, Jason craved the hands-on excitement of real estate investing and felt ready for his next challenge. He elected to sell off his share of the company to his business partner and return to his true passion for real estate sales and investing.

As a successful entrepreneur, Jason´s main business focus is on his clients being Buyers, tenant buyers, lenders and Joint Venture partners and their real estate success. Whether it be buying or selling their homes, helping them break into the rental market with an investment property, or facilitat-ing commercial transactions, Jason is committed to ensuring his clients end up on top with the best possible results. Jason enjoys spending countless hours learning all he can to better his businesses and learning new skills to outperform market conditions and trends in his field.

At the time of this writing Jason personally bought, invested, financed, flipped or coached over 72 creative real estate deals in the prior 17 months alone.

Jason invites you to contact him directly by either phone: (403)-804-3150, Fax: (866)300-3255, or email: Jason@thewatsongroup.com for further advice, clarification, or investment opportunities.

CHAPTER 12

Seller-Financing

New and Improved for the 21st Century

By David Thomas, MD

My friend, Ron LeGrand, always said houses are easy to sell if you buy the right house, attract the right buyer and make it easy for them to buy. Well, duh! It sounds too simple and obvious at first glance, but when the issue of selling houses is examined, that is what it all boils down to. Attracting the right buyer and making it easy for them to buy is what seller financing is all about. Seller financing has been around for as long as people have been buying and selling real estate. Its popularity and prevalence has varied with the real estate market condition, but it has always been in the quiver of tools for the professional real estate investor.

Seller financing was used frequently and effectively in the late 1970's and 1980's when mortgage interest rates were high – running in the range of 12-18% due to the relatively low supply of money to lend. It was tough for buyers to get an affordable mortgage and that made it tough for homeowners to sell. Today's real estate market condition is different from yesteryear. In spite of mortgage interest rates being at historical low levels and banks having plenty of money to lend, buyers are having difficulty obtaining a mortgage because mortgage companies have tightened lending requirements. This, coupled with the overabundance of houses for sale, has resulted in a similar effect to yesteryear in that it is tougher for homeowners to sell their house; well, for the uneducated it is.

Seller financing does not mean the seller cannot cash out and has to carry a mortgage for years. In fact the Federal government does not want you to do that unless you are a registered mortgage broker. Due to mortgage fraud and irregularities, they passed the Secure and Fair Enforcement Mortgage Licensing Act in 2008 (SAFE Act) and required every state to pass their own version of the SAFE Act within two years. Now, I must inform you that I am not an attorney and am not giving legal opinion or advice. I have done research and have discussed this with my attorney, and you should too.

THE SAFE ACT DOES HAVE SAFE HARBORS WHERE SELLER FINANCING IS OK.

1. Non-residential property (commercial and multi-family buildings greater than 4 units)

2. Where the buyer is a real estate investor

3. Where the owner-occupant is selling the house

4. Where a close relative is selling the house (parents, off-spring and siblings are OK. Aunts, uncles and cousins are not OK)

The SAFE Act applies to single family homes, condominiums, cooperative units, mobile homes, trailers, manufactured homes, recreational vehicles, houseboats, and residential lots.

This law, not surprisingly, has had unintended results on seller financing. HUD recognized this and said they would clarify. Real estate professionals, lenders and investors eagerly awaited this "clarification." HUD issued this in June 2011,

"An individual required to be licensed under the SAFE Act is an individual who is engaged in the 'business of a loan originator'; that is, an individual who acts as a residential mortgage loan originator

with respect to financing that is provided in a commercial context and with some degree of habitualness or repetition." [1]

Now isn't that as clear as chocolate milk. Certainly, owner financing by a real estate investor is in a commercial context, but what constitutes "habitualness" and over what period of time? Your guess is as good as theirs. The only thing I can suggest here is to contact your state department of financial institutions, and ask them what is the definition of "habitualness."

Penalties for violation of the SAFE Act include: $25,000 penalty for each violation and inability to collect interest on the mortgage.

When real estate is sold with financing, there are three documents:

1. The Promissory Note is an IOU where the buyer borrows money from a lender and agrees to pay them in the future.

2. The Deed, which states the ownership of the real estate. These two documents are independent of each other.

3. The Mortgage, which links the Promissory Note to the real estate in the form of a lien or encumbrance. The SAFE Act governs these mortgages.

Fear not; real estate entrepreneurs are a creative bunch who, when faced with adversity, will achieve their objective by legal, ethical means. The solution is to not sell real estate; sell an entity where real estate is the sole asset of the entity – be it a land trust, LLC, or limited partnership. This changes the nature of the sale from <u>real</u> property to <u>personal</u> property, in the case of a trust, corporation in the case of an LLC, or partnership in the limited partnership. The terms of the sale will be in the form of a contract transferring personal property from one party to another. There is no mortgage, so the SAFE Act does not come into play.

It's time for an example, and we'll use the land trust. A short sale on a nice house in an OK neighborhood was negotiated for $55,000. We found a buyer at $90,000, and he has $15,000 cash down payment. The buyer has one of those prequalification letters that are more useful in the bathroom than in a business transaction. The buyer could not qualify for a mortgage because they paid cash for everything and had no established credit, thus had an inadequate credit score even though they have sufficient income and low expenses. The $15,000 down payment is 16% of the purchase price. These facts make me feel comfortable proceeding with the deal.

My attorney closes the short sale with the buyer being the 123 Main Street Land Trust. A Land Trust is a document about 13 pages long stating the rights, interests and duties of the two parties involved: the Trustee and the Beneficiary. The Trustee functions as a business manager in that he signs all the documents for buying, managing, and selling the property. The Trustee manages the Trust for the benefit of the Beneficiaries. The Land Trust Agreement is <u>NEVER</u> recorded at your county courthouse. The 123 Main Street Land Trust owns the house. The Trustee is my Property Management LLC. (An LLC can be a trustee in my state. You need to see if your state permits this.) The beneficiary is My Buying LLC, 100% interest in the Trust. Normal enough, right? Now for the new twist. My attorney has created a contract where My Buying LLC is selling its beneficial interest in the 123 Main Street Trust. The beneficial interest is personal property; not real property and not subject to the SAFE Act. The contract dictates the terms of the sale. In this case, the buyer gets 1% of the beneficial interest and My Buying LLC retains 99% interest until 360 payments of $550.00 are made. The exact payment requirements are to be negotiated with your buyer. There could be a number of payments for a time then a balloon payment for the balance due. Other terms of the contract that should be included cover rights and responsibilities of each party: buyer may occupy the property of the trust as long as payments remain current, buyer shall maintain the trust property in good and habitable condition at his own expense, trustee shall maintain hazard and fire insurance, trustee shall pay property tax, method to resolve any dispute between the beneficiaries, default in payments by buyer, etc. Your attorney should be adept at contract law so as as to cover these issues and contingencies with sufficient legalese to protect your interest. You remain in control until all terms of the contract are met by the buyer.

A brief word about the trust agreement; the trust must have language concerning the rights and interests of the beneficiaries including the right to direct the Trustee to convey the title to the Trust Property, right to manage and control the Trust Property. This is important; after enumerating the rights and interests of the beneficiaries, language should be present stating:

"The foregoing rights shall be deemed to be personal property and may be assigned and otherwise transferred as such. No Beneficiary shall have any legal or equitable right, title or interest, as realty, in or to any real estate held in trust under this Agreement."

Wow, those are powerful words. Reread them. They are from Ron LeGrand's Land Trust Agreement. Spells it out plainly, doesn't it. The beneficiaries do not have legal ownership of the real estate, and any interest they have in the Trust is personal property. No sale of real estate, no mortgage, no SAFE Act. It's a beautiful thing, elegant in its crafting.

When using an LLC for one of these transactions, the house is the only asset of the LLC. Let's reiterate; set up a separate LLC for each house. The buyer will be made a Member of the LLC and has a very small minority interest in the LLC. You would be the Managing Member of the LLC and maintain control. Your lawyer will create a contract for selling your interest to the buyer that should be very similar to the contract discussed in the Land Trust section in addressing pertinent issues and contingencies.

The Limited Partnership is very similar in that the buyer is a limited partner with a small minority interest in the partnership, and you maintain general partnership and control. You may or may not elect to have a limited partnership interest as well. Again, your lawyer's contract will dictate the transfer of interest to the buyer.

Earlier, I said that you do not have to wait for years to get your money. In the above example, the land trust borrowed $75,000 from a private lender. She was willing to accept payments over time of $550.00 amortized for 30 years at 8% interest. $55,000 of the $75,000 was used to fund the short sale closing.

Selling Price of Beneficial interest	$90,000.00
Down Payment	-$15,000.00
Balance due	$75,000.00
Short Sale	-$55,000.00
Closing Cost, Legal Fees, etc.	-$5,000.00
Balance	$15,000.00

My Buying LLC receives the $15,000 down payment and the $15,000 balance. Not a bad deal, and everyone involved comes away with something. This is what entrepreneurs do best. Creatively solve challenges.

I hope this has been helpful and has stirred some interest in real estate. I applaud your investment in your education. From my practice of medicine, I realized early on that learning is a life-long process. Who would want a surgeon operating on a family member who had not gained any new knowledge in technique or treatments since graduating 15 years ago? That physician would be doing a disservice to his patient as well as himself and his family. The same holds true in any area of life. Market conditions change, laws change, procedures change, but the basic transaction remains the same. Knowledge and creativity are the means to get the task accomplished. I wish you well in your future endeavors.

1 *Federal Register: Vol. 76, No. 126*, page 38465, June 30, 2011.

About David

David A. Thomas, MD is an Eagle Scout and a Board Certified anesthesiologist who practiced for 12 years at Jewish Hospital in Louisville, KY and "retired" from that in 2006 and has been a full time investor since then. He grew up in a family that was a buy and hold real estate investment family – working his way through high school, college and medical school by working on his parents' rental property.

David decided in high school to invest in real estate for the long term and to use a medical practice as a springboard for this. His first investment in real estate was in 1986 during medical school – investing in a duplex with his parents. David and his young family lived in one unit, and he helped his father convert the attic to a one-bedroom apartment. The fuse had been lit. Later, he and his wife Becky have owned and managed as many as 105 apartments, townhouses, condos, and houses at one time. David and Becky have four daughter who worked on their rental properties just as he had done with his parents.

Dr. Dave, as he in known, has appeared in Business First, and is a real estate coach and speaker sharing the stage with gurus Ron LeGrand and Jeff Kaller. He is an active member of the Kentuckiana Real Estate Investor's Association (KREIA), giving presentations on Low Income Tax Credit Projects and Short Sales. He has hosted a number of the nationally acclaimed Learn On The Site (LOTS) Programs for KREIA. See KREIA.com for details.

Dr. Dave can be contacted at realestatedoc451@aol.com

CHAPTER 13

The Real Estate Reality Show

By Joel Sangerman

It was the HOT summer of 1996 in Chicago. Trang, my sweet-sexy Asian girlfriend, and I were amidst a crowd of onlookers at North Avenue Beach enjoying the annual Air and Water Show. We watched the Blue Angels race through the clear blue skies as I mentally committed to making big money in real estate. This would be in addition to a generous salary from a career in the pharmaceutical industry. Legal pharmaceuticals of course!

I had dreams of producing "seed money" for another venture. Quick and easy real estate profits would be a means to 'rake in' investment capital. I dreamed of using the cash I would earn to launch a Caribbean-island-based Internet sports book. Trang would be by my side mixing delicious mai-tais that only she could make. We called it Wopatooyu punch because they really whopped it to you! Starlit nights in the Island's sports office would be spent watching the Chicago Bulls continue their run of championships. Morning hangovers would be nursed whilst counting the profits from the "10% juice" we would earn from myriads of global sports-betters.

Ultimately, it was a good thing that I did not pursue that dream in exactly that fashion. Like-minded dreamers who did set off to the Islands to earn millions from sports book operations are either in jail now, have been murdered by thugs, or are effectively banned from the great United States of America for violating our gambling laws.

Enter – A slightly revised dream: Do real estate deals, continue a great career, and relocate to Las Vegas to capitalize on what seemed like a no-brainer – the rapid growth of Las Vegas real estate. I'll take Boom Town for $1000, Alex!

It was the perfect plan. I studied real estate like a mad man for about six months. If you did not want to talk about real estate you did not want to talk to me. I lived, ate, and breathed every book, every text, and every manual I could on how to make money in real estate. I voraciously consumed tape cassettes of trainings and attended several live "boot camps." I was afraid to pull the trigger on doing a deal until I knew everything I possibly could. Soon, I could talk all of the talk, but I could not walk much of the walk.

I specifically remember flying to a corporate sales meeting in Hawaii. That is how we "rolled" in the pharmaceutical industry back in those days. I had Ron LeGrand's Fast Cash Generator Paperback and tapes with me for the flight. Man, when I got done with my first exposures to Ron's system I was ready. I came back from Hawaii and booked a trip for Trang and myself to take 90 days later in Jamaica. I just knew that by then, I would have bought and sold my first investment property – garnering at least a $10,000 profit to pay for our trip and more.

It actually happened. Beginners luck, big time!! I made a ridiculously low offer on an REO condo owned by Fannie Mae (FNMA). I went directly to the listing Realtor explaining that if she convinced FNMA to take my offer, her commission would actually be better than if she sold it for full price to someone else. She made the offer but did not seem to care and neither did FNMA. A couple weeks later she called back saying FNMA was willing to go to a number that was exactly my M-A-O, "maximum allowable offer," per the strategies I had learned. I didn't mess around coun-tering it. Jamaican Red Stripe, all-inclusive buffets, and parasail-ing were on the other side of getting this deal done.

I signed the contract the same day that Florida beat Florida State in the Sugar bowl, winning a cool $1,000. Well, I thought Florida was my big winner for the day. Wrong!! FNMA was my big winner, as the resale of that property netted over $30,000 in cash profit.

My lawyer, an ex-Miami Dolphin, closed the sale in a confer-ence room of a downtown Chicago title company, while I sipped Pina-Coladas and listened to Ron LeGrand tapes on a Sony Walkman.

The only bad part of that story was that before heading out to Jamaica I stupidly went to a tanning bed and burnt myself red as a lobster. Trang and I had made a not-so-gentlemanly bet on who could tan the darkest and I wanted to sneak a head start. Believe me, laughing at the jokes Ron told during his taped seminars was painful in the belly and to burnt skin. Good times for sure though! It is pretty hard to be upset when you have a $30,000 payday waiting for you at home earned with virtually no effort. Like I said, beginners luck!

Well, talk about a fire being lit underneath the fanny! I worked tirelessly trying to replicate that early success. Ummmmm, not so easy. Pissing Realtors off, having sellers tell to me to go "F" myself, auction prices being bid up to retail, and questioning how successful I could be, all invaded my real estate "mojo" for weeks on end.

I traveled to a seminar held in a not-so-luxurious Cleveland ho-tel for some re-motivation. The greatest lesson learned there was on the value of having the mindset of "some will, some won't, so what, …NEXT!" From there it was Next, Next, Next, Next all the way until Marcia from Michigan called me on my "I Buy Houses" advertisement in the Chicago Tribune. I started off as the only one in the Chicago Tribune with that ad. Amazing. Within a few months there were about six of those ads in the Second City's major newspaper.

Marcia had a property that I bought on an option contract for $30,000 with my buyers $50,000. That was 1997, and today that property is probably worth a couple hundred thousand dollars. Hmmm, $20,000 today or hold it and rent it and make exponentially more 15 years later? Hindsight: it is definitely 20/20. At the same time, speaking of 20/20, $20k large isn't a bad payday either! That is, unless you are a cocky 29 year old who decided to leverage real estate profits and trade stock options. Fast-paced fun with a lot of highs and lows, … but OOOOOPS! Greed will win you some and can lose you a lot. For me it was both – in exactly that order. I decided that going forward I would pretty much stick with real estate and the burgeoning career I enjoyed that always served me well.

The next two deals were like Bang, Bang! Sterling got an inheritance that he wanted to use to help fund his crack habit. (Presumed after meeting him.) He sold me his Mom's south side bungalow worth $100,000 for $60,000. After cutting myself bloody on broken glass pipes in the basement trying to help the junk guy get the house cleaned out, I decided I'd let the experts do the expert's work. Waldamar, my junk guy, cleaned the hell out of that house!

I advertised the fixed-up home for sale aggressively. Among the plethora of cold-calling Realtors came Jamez, a Jheri curl-wearing smooth talker from Chicago's south side who looked like an Eddie Murphy character but spoke like the president. He said he'd have it sold in a couple weeks for top dollar. I gave him a try and like clockwork, three days later, he produced a sweet contract for full price that netted $15,000 cash. I think Snagglepuss said it best, "Heavens to Mergatroid! Exit stage left, even!"

Next was the sweetest little old lady from Skokie who unfortunately lost her husband and could not bear the memories of living there without him. She wanted out immediately. She also wanted more than the M-A-O. Well, how was I going to give her $120,000 on her $160,000 house and get her out of there and down to Florida to be with relatives?

This was so cool. Cool literally and figuratively because it was a cold winter in Chicago. She quit claim deeded the house to me, and I also gave her one back for escrow as security guaranteeing my performance. I refinanced it at 80% of $160,000 netting $128,000. She got $120,000 to terminate the quit claim deed that was held in escrow. I kept the rest for holding costs while I tried to sell it. Well, my intent was to use it for holding costs anyway. My pattern was, "got cash? Let's gamble!"

The music was thumping while driving north to the Oneida Casino in Green Bay, Wisconsin. While doubling down my A-7 against the dealer 6, I learned from a friend who was helping stage the house for resale that the pipes had burst during a -25 degree wind-chill day in Chicago.

Cold water was gushing everywhere as I raced southbound on 43 with "Packer green and yellow" blackjack chips stuffed in my pockets. Where in the world was the shut off valve ?! Luckily, we found a plumber to help that very day. Also, fortuitous was the fact that my good friend Ray from Canada was moving down to Chicago to work in the pharmaceutical corporate offices of my day job. He wanted to buy a house and he was not real picky. I ended up giving Ray the Canadian a great deal that still created almost $25,000 in profit. Ray didn't care about frozen water and pipes. He was a Saskatchewan boy, and it was "no problem, eh !"

Now what I did not mention was the great personal tragedy that happened after returning from Jamaica with Trang. I used to affectionately call her Mae Ling after a saucy-minx like character in a Bruce Lee movie. Anyway, Mae Ling did not like cats. Well, my Mom died a few years earlier and I had three cats I promised to take care of. I learned to love cat pee as part of the real estate game, which is a whole other story involving Inez, but I sure did not like the occasionally intolerable smell of cats fuming through my beautiful "Bucktown" house in Chicago. Neither did Mae Ling. But it got much worse than cat odor.

I loved Mae Ling like no one I had ever loved. She was everything to me and she was the best of the best. She had a very bad asthma attack one night in the middle of the night and decided to drive home. She did not get far before she called me totally out of breath …. and click. No Mae Ling on the phone, and no Mae Ling to answer my call backs. Was she dead on the highway? I didn't know, but I searched at least a dozen local hospitals and called police all over trying to see if she crashed somewhere on the way home. I found her at Resurrection hospital in Chicago. Now she was Jane Doe, because no one found her purse. She had a breathing machine breathing for her. That was very, very sad to see. Long story short, she survived. Yes, she did survive, but that was an experience that changed a lot of things for her and ultimately ended our love affair. I was tore up. And I was tore up good with sorrow and depression over losing her. There is a point in telling that story but for now, back to Real Estate.

Inez had cats too. As I stated, one thing the great Ron LeGrand will teach you is to love the smell of cat pee when it comes to buying real estate. If a house smells like cats you can reek havoc on the asking price. That is exactly what I did. Inez was stubborn though. She wanted her price of $60,000 and did not like my offer of $40,000 cash at all. The house was worth $60,000 so we settled on $60,000. How did I make money on that? I broke out Cam Dunlap's financial calculator, the trusty TI-BA35, and we wrote the following out on a yellow legal pad. "$30,000 CASH plus $30,000 paid over 100 months at $300 per month." This would be part of her "retirement plan." She wanted to move to a trailer in Florida – which she did. Sunny Acres or something, I think.

If you have not figured it out yet, this is effectively a zero interest loan that was not even secured by a lien on the house. This allowed me to finance as I pleased while still owing her the unsecured debt. I paid her every month for all 100 months but in the first 3 months she needed more cash. So I bought $10,000 of the note back for $4000 cash. As I recall, she needed to get her son out of the slammer for some sort of bad deed. He did not look handsome in pinstripes nor in orange jumpsuits, as she explained it.

Are you guys getting the point here?

The reality is that real estate is easy on paper. In real life, though, things happen to you, and things happen to your homes, and you deal with real people with real problems. That is why real estate is not as simple and easy as it is made out to be on almost all TV infomercials, seminars, books, and manuals.

Of course, it is definitely a great way to make money. Actually, it may be one of the best ways. But let's just be real and know and accept that most of the time there is more to it than making lowball offers until one gets accepted so you can flip for a big profit and take off to the Caribbean.

Essentially, successful real estate investing takes 5 key traits: Basic business sense, the ability to communicate clearly, the patience to educate yourself, the initiative to take action, and the willingness to take carefully-calculated risks.

Once you have those elements ingrained into the very fiber of your being, you will likely win and you will likely win big.

Here are some blurbs of my favorite other "reality real estate" parables:

- The guy on Ellen Street who was being evicted. On a whim I went to check on the property to see if he left. He did. He also left a burning fire for me in the living room, which I was able to put out before it got bad. Talk about fortunate timing. He did not like me much apparently. I guess eviction will do that to you.

- The New York Cop who moved in to my Las Vegas

condo and got himself evicted. In Vegas, it is like the Wild, Wild West. If you don't pay, you can't stay. After a few days, you can lock them out, and after 30 days you can even keep their stuff if they don't claim it. I'm still thinking about putting his NYC cop stuff on Ebay but I like it better as a Real Estate war story souvenir.

• Janice, the Las Vegas buyer who was represented by a fast talking Realtor and loan officer. They offered $860,000 for the condo I bought for $626,000. This was above my list price and not unheard of in a rapidly-escalating market. The contract called for a 7% agent fee and 3% points on the buyer's loan to be paid by me. It looked great to me. On $234,000 of spread, a lot can be done. Janice was foreclosed on 18 months later. It may have been a great deal for her, considering I suspect she was a "homeless" person prior to buying the condo.

In 2008, the US housing market was in the midst of the greatest collapse ever; hit especially hard was Las Vegas. I read an article in the Las Vegas Sun describing a process I suspect may have happened with Janice. Unscrupulous professionals would use a homeless person with good credit as a "straw" buyer. A "no documentation," "no income verification," (aka "liar") loan at 100% financing is arranged. The deal is closed and the homeless person is no longer homeless. They will never be able to actually pay the mortgage, but it will take a very long time before they can be foreclosed and evicted. The "dealmakers" would walk with big commissions. The article suggested these real estate bandits would simultaneously run 25 previously homeless people through their system at a time. On $860,000 condos that would be about $86,000 each. Multiply that by 25 and you get $2.15 Million.

At that time, the market in Las Vegas was up, up and away, and showed no sign of ever turning back. Boy, …was that wrong! Thank goodness I did not rent that place like I thought I might. Today that $860,000 condo is worth about $225,000. P-h-e-w-w-w!

One of the houses I now own that I am keeping, is on a beautiful golf course with a panoramic Las Vegas strip view. It was last sold for $850,000. It was sold to me in 2010 for $349,000 as an REO from our good friends at Bank of America who picked up all Countrywide's dead assets including this one.

I am also keeping the wakeboard boat and the Illinois lake house that my family of seven will use in the summer. There is a private beach that reminds me of that North Avenue Air Show in 1996. Best of all, Trang and I eventually reunited. Now we can enjoy fantasizing with our 5 kids aged 7,6,5,4, and 2. This time it won't be about Caribbean sports books but something more like Euro-Disney Land!

In writing this, all of these experiences played back in my head like a Real Estate Reality Show Series. Unlike "The Bachelor," none of the players got roses or rings at the closings. However, they did get a prize. They got a solution.

Here is a bold statement: A deal can be structured to make money in almost every real estate situation. If that is true, then there should be no house where an offer could not be made to a seller. When that can be done confidently and competently, extreme efficiency is realized in what sometimes can be a numbers game. Remember, "some will, some won't, so what, …Next!" Giving any seller the chance to "will" or to "won't" depends on making offers. Simply put, the more offers you make without being limited to one type of offer, the better the chances are to lock up winning deals.

Your time has value. Making the most of your time talking to sellers means you have to have more than one way 'to skin the cat.' It doesn't matter how you skin the cat as long as that cat looks bald when you're done. But cats have created problems for me, so let's just call it what I think Ron used to call it ….. Become a "Transaction Engineer." This means learning the specific needs of the seller (or buyer) and tapping the knowledge base that includes an array of options to structure a winning deal. This can be achieved through education.

Read, listen, read again, listen again, align with mentors and coaches, re-read, listen to seminars again, and bounce questions, ideas, and thoughts off coaches who have been there. Having a coach calibrate your thinking through the lens of their experience can be priceless. It can pay huge dividends in preparation and in sweetening deals already on the table.

If help is needed, if questions need answers through dialogue, if there is fear or trepidation, or if this idea of "calibrating" strategy is something you would like to discuss, please feel free to contact me by email at joel@ibuyrealestate.com so we can schedule time to talk live. I would be glad to help in any way I can.

About Joel

Joel Sangerman is a dedicated professional in the field of healthcare economics. He began investing in real estate as an asset diversification strategy in the 1990's. In 1997, Joel formed DMC Equities, Inc. and began buying and selling properties in Chicago with later expansion to Las Vegas. Closing his first $10 million in real estate deals, using many different types of purchase and sale methods, refined his expertise across several different investment strategies. Joel was awarded the Editors Choice Award in 2011 for his work in the best selling business book, *"Trendsetters."* His candid stock market views, coupled with innovative methods for using self directed IRAs to diversify and profit in real estate, helped launch *"Trendsetters"* to best seller status at Amazon. Being interviewed for blockbuster real estate educational courses and being included as a contributing author in *"Sold"* are great honors – given his approach to real estate investing has been secondary to an exciting corporate career.

In the spirit of what Joel calls "personal bandwidth," he is currently applying some of the same creative business skills honed in the real estate arena to the pursuit of improving the nation's healthcare delivery system. Joel is one of many dynamic leaders participating in the national discussion on healthcare payment reforms that will revolutionize healthcare delivery in the USA over the next few years. This dual passion for career and entrepreneurial pursuit is what drives Joel's success in both endeavors. Being able to operate successfully on a part-time basis is one of the major benefits of adding real estate investment to a portfolio of life activities. Joel has counseled hundreds of friends, colleagues, and contacts on developing the multi-tasking ability to accomplish real estate success without compromising careers or involvement in other passions. Joel offers specialized coaching to new real estate investors with a no-nonsense approach. On a larger and less personal scale, Joel is a highly engaging public speaker taking the podium at various real estate investment conferences and healthcare industry meetings.

For a limited time, several bonuses are available to readers of *"SOLD"* who may desire help in the following areas:

1. Setting up self-directed IRAs and opportunities for low-risk,

high-yielding real estate investments

2. Not-for-profit groups and organizations may inquire about booking "no fee" speaking engagements.

3. No-charge consultations on real estate matters may be scheduled on a limited basis

4. There is tremendous need throughout the country for homeowners to get competent help navigating the process of selling their homes as a "short sale" or in modifying existing loans to be more affordable. This is a highly specialized area of real estate that is evolving and ever changing. Joel will take a personal interest in helping homeowners needing this sort of help.

5. Joel is authoring a new "reality" book and DVD series and is recruiting participants. Inquiries from *"SOLD"* readers about participating in this exciting and unique project are welcome.

Please feel free to contact Joel directly through his website at:
www.ibuyrealestate.com or
via email at joel@ibuyrealestate.com.
Live assistance may be obtained at 702-364-2323.

CHAPTER 14

Real Estate Marketing Secret "Smoking Gun"

By Christine Rae

As the author of *Home Staging For Dummies®*, I can honestly say <u>real estate staging is for smart people</u>™. Smart sellers, smart buyers, smart real estate agents, smart investors, smart renovators, smart bankers, smart estate executors, etc., etc., etc.

What I know for sure is home staging is the most under-utilized and under-valued service in the process of selling real estate. Millions of sellers and thousands of agents every day leave money on the table by not using the service at all, or by using it incorrectly. People want cheap and fast solutions to condition items they have ignored for years; what they are not comprehending is today's buyer has a much different mindset than buyers of years gone by. Buyers today are busy; the purchase of property is probably the biggest investment most people make, however they do not invest a reciprocal amount of time in selecting the purchase.

In fact, statistics show that 93% of buyers look on the Internet first to make a list of properties they want to consider. Making a list of 10, 74% of those people will drive by the property first, before contacting an agent or seller (and half will do it at night). What that means to you as a seller/agent is, (a). your site better be found, (b). there needs to be really great photos which sell the features – not show how the current people live, (c). the curb appeal is what keeps a property on the "to see" list, and (d). the experience when they see it has to exceed expectations.

Failure to do so will result in prospective buyers moving on or offering 'less than' sale price. Most buyers take less than five minutes to tour property; wherever the eye rests the sale begins. What that means is professional staging is a strategy not decoration.

Five things influence the sale of property and excellent staging professionals affect all of them: Price, Location, Size, Condition and Staging.

(1). Price:

This is the first filter; buyers generally don't look at property priced outside of the bar of their mortgage ability. Therefore establishing a sale price outside of current market analysis is a dangerous game. An overpriced property can be missed on the first filter. Ultimately, a property will only sell for what a buyer is willing to pay. Stagers are not involved in the pricing of property – that is left to a real estate expert. However, the work that stagers do illustrates the value of the property and supports the price.

(2 & 3). Location and Size:

78% of a decision to look at a property is based on these two factors.

Generally, people know where they want to live in terms of an environmental footprint; for example, close to shops, schools, dining or waterfront, country, downtown, etc. Properties in the price range they can afford, but outside where they want to live, are discounted (of course, they may be revisited with the hope of offering less, if the first choices fail to inspire purchase).

Size, as in sq. footage and dimensions of rooms, then become the deciding factor for entry onto the "Must See" list. Stagers enhance location and maximize size of space.

(4). Condition:

This is such a vital part of selling at the maximum price point; often confused with staging. Staging is not condition; condition is deferred maintenance. All the things a seller didn't do during the time they lived in the house. The cracks, the dust and dirt, old fixtures, painting, upgrading, landscaping - pretty well anything which should have been done, will need to be done before the house is marketed if maximum price is to be achieved. This is often the stumbling block for agents, because in the rush to market and honour MLS rules, they do not or cannot allow enough time for the property to be properly readied for sale.

It's like selling a car without washing it, fixing it up, etc. and expecting to get full price – doesn't work. People buy emotionally then support their decision intellectually. If a property is in need of work (haven't met a house which doesn't), it doesn't serve the seller best by saying, "it doesn't matter," "just do what you can," "focus on major rooms," or "Oh! Its just the office coming through – they are agents, they know."

Baloney – those agents are people too and they remember everything they see – and they won't come back to see it when or if you get it sale ready. My solution for this is simple: get seller approval to defer showings until its ready, then make a stipulation at the bottom of contract "No showings until after ___" (...insert date). Allow the time necessary to get the house ready for sale.

Another successful way to manage the situation is to take the listing as exclusive first; that way the agent is in charge of who and when showings are conducted. An agent can honour the broker rules by reporting the listing and honour the home owner by not marketing and not showing the property until the sellers have it in tip-top condition. When the time is right, complete the paperwork to put it on the MLS and start bringing the office through. In our experience, a fully-staged property goes under contract in at least half if not less than half of the time an unstaged property sells – without reducing price and often with offers over asking.

(5) Showcase Staging:

A recent example: a property in a metropolitan area, sellers anxious to sell. After 40 years, they were retiring to the South and wanted to secure the most money possible. As you know, house prices 40 years ago were way less than today, so realistically, a significant amount over what they paid would be a great ROI. They paid $48,000 – today, houses in their area were going for $780,000, so the temptation is to bring the property to market "as is", even if the sale price isn't maximized, the sellers will still be happy.

The proviso, of course, will always be in what time frame and at what price. Fortunately the sellers hired a market savvy agent who recommended working with a certified staging professional. A staging consultation is a very wise investment; in addition to addressing condition a good stager will always recommend a pre-sale home inspection to assess condition of items within the property outside of the scope of expertise of a stager (like furnace, roof, damp, etc.). The stager reviewed each room and compiled recommendations which were discussed with the seller and agent, budget and time were discussed and work was completed. The time frame to address the condition was two weeks.

The stager then "showcased" each room. The people I teach and certify are taught when styling rooms, to target the buyer most likely to purchase the property. So in this case, some furniture and accessories were rented to supplement what the homeowner had. Time: one day.

Agent brought the office through, and offers were on the table by end of day. The sellers accepted an offer in less than three days on the market for $1.1m. Was it worth the time and effort? The sellers certainly think so, and the agent is enjoying the success, reduced DOM, increased referrals, less stress, reduced marketing efforts and extra commission.

Showcase Staging works! It is not decorating, it is marketing!

My company (CSP International) conducted a survey over a two year period. We asked Real Estate professionals "how important do you think staging is, in the process of selling property?" 98% of them said "it's vital." Interestingly, when we asked them if they had used staging, or talked about staging with their clients, less than 20% of them had. So, asking the obvious question: "Why, when you acknowledge it is a vital component for sale, have you not done something about it?"

The majority said they didn't know how to effectively speak on the subject, didn't have supporting material, didn't know how to communicate the message or how to discern "what good staging is; what constitutes excellence in the field and how much it would cost." Ok, decent enough reasons, but, in my book, certainly not excusable.

Selling real estate is a stressful time for most buyers; they want to be sure they hired the right agent, who will work on their behalf to secure the most money possible. There is no reason today for an agent to not recommend staging services to sellers – much like they recommend a home inspection, title search or other related services connected to selling property. To support agent education, I hired a real estate agent with 33 years experience as a technical advisor to develop a training program specifically to address all those issues/concerns they have. Even so, in our experience, the majority of agents don't want to pay for the training. What I hear from them is "I won't take it if it doesn't have educational credits. Now, if there are agents who are not interested in educating themselves, in order to service their clients, then it is as a systemic problem within the real estate industry which needs to be fixed.

CSP International has secured CEC for the program in many states (example - California granted eight) but I can tell you - it is an expensive and arduous process without any guarantees. *Much like the Jay Kinder and Michael Reece program for real estate agents who want to be successful agents,* CSP International focuses our efforts on training agents who want to be the best in their industry, earning the prestigious "CSP Elite" agent (www.cspelite.com) to provide better service to clients, and not agents who are looking for credits in order to hang on to their license.

HomeGain (www.homegain.com) conducts annual surveys measuring real estate agents opinions for ROI of certain services connected to selling real estate. The result for staging over the last three years: it has grown exponentially. In 2008, it was 169%; 2009, it was 349% and in 2010 the results were a staggering 586% ROI. What does that mean? It means over the years, as real estate agents have seen the magic performed by stagers, they have changed their opinion of the results this service provides. It doesn't remove the challenges I referred to earlier, but it is a great statistic to work with.

Maritz Research also provides some excellent statistics to help bolster the cause: 79% of sellers are willing to invest up to $5,000 in getting their property sale-ready if they knew what to do. Guess what? Stagers know how to use that budget for maximum appeal. 63% of buyers are willing to pay more money for a house which is "move in" ready; wow… graduates of my program (CSP) know how to target the buyer who is most likely to purchase the property. With these three stats, you would think people would be convinced! After all, it isn't rocket science to see the value of staging property before sale. Even so, people struggle with spending money on property they are going to be leaving. The problem here is the use of the word SPENDING. It is a word often associated with waste. Using *investment* instead tells a different tale and one where the message is return on investment (ROI) – much more appealing. Interestingly, the majority of the 63% who said they would be willing to pay more money for a house which was "move-in" ready – were men! Do you think that is because they do not want to inherit the "Honey Do" list from the preceding owner?

Both sides of the equation boil down to "Time, Work and Money." Sellers say we don't have the money or the time and buyers say we don't have the time, don't want to do the work and we don't have the money. The quintessential fact which is so often overlooked is that today's buyer is not the buyer of yesteryear. They are usually younger than today's sellers. The younger demographic are less patient, less tolerant and have high expectations (which have been set by an over-indulgent baby-boomer generation). Today's young buyer expects to live in a house at least at the level of the house they lived in with their parents. They are bombarded by media-influencing thoughts around design, move-in ready, investments, and the end of the world – short life, bank collapses, Medicare concerns – they want to live now! "Move In" ready property sells first, because it is easy for them to do!

Who Pays? Ah ha! The proverbial question!

The short answer is the seller pays!

The seller created the situation, the seller stands to gain the most and ultimately it is the seller's decision; however, a real estate agent who accepts a listing where the seller is unwilling to affect condition is courting a rod for his/her own back. The listing will sit, and if it sells, will sell for less than the seller wants – which leaves a bad impression with the seller of the efforts the agent made to get the property sold. If it doesn't sell, it sends a totally different message to all the people who see the agent's sign on the lawn! You might think people know the house isn't selling because of price or condition, but perception is everything and the subliminal message is: "this agent failed to sell this house."

Some market savvy agents have redirected marketing dollars to invest in having a stager conduct the "consultation." I refer to the consultation as the road map for market- readying the property. When you work with a great stager who has excellent communication skills, she/he is able to tell the seller what needs to be done without creating any bad feelings, and in a way the seller understands the value of what is shared. In the event the seller is unwilling to do any or all of the recommendations, the seller can never say the agent was negligent in their duties. It was the seller who decided not to 'ready' the property, and ultimately, it is the seller who will accept offers less than he/she expected – but at least they know the agent did his/her best.

Just as a Doctor signs a Hippocratic oath to "do no harm," a real estate agent has a fiduciary responsibility to the client to do the very best he/she can to support the sale of property. Knowing about a service which will facilitate not just the expediency of sale, but secure the best return on their client's largest investment AND not telling is totally irresponsible in my opinion. There are no excuses. Ask yourself this: Is what you are doing today for your client improving or taking away service?

Make the moves necessary to do the work for improved client services today! What I know for sure is, if you don't….. your competition will!

About Christine

Christine Rae is known as the leading expert and trend-setter of the Real Estate Staging Industry. In her role as President and CEO for CSP International, she steered the company to the top of the excellence chart for her industry. The CSP International Academy is known as a successful incubator for 'would be' entrepreneurs with a decorating flair who want control over their own destiny, while building successful, profitable businesses of their own. CSP International provides a safe haven for learning, support, knowledge, best practices and leading market trends. Graduates from the Academy benefit from a reputation of excellence, helping them gain credibility and recognition as they market and develop their own business.

Christine is recognized as the world's leading authority on staging from her global experience, as well as through her work in developing standards, examinations, professionalism and trend forecasting. She is the author of *Home Staging for Dummies®* (Wiley press), editor of the world's only Staging Industry Magazine, and is co-authoring two new books in the works for release early 2012: *The Best Business Book You Will Ever Need* and *Nothing But Net.*

Christine developed and trademarked EcoStaging®. She is an Industry Expert Blogger for REALTOR® magazine, a regular contributor to Real Estate Magazine and is the Green Staging Expert for HomeGain®. She has been a featured speaker and keynote for many industry events including six Stagers Expo's, Real Estate Staging Association, Sydney, Australia Real Estate event, and expert speaker at the California Association of Realtors convention. Christine and her unique, signature CSP® Real Estate Staging Business Program is accredited through RESA and she has received awards, accolades, and recognition — including Innovator of the Year. In January 2012 she was presented with the prestigious Lifetime Achievement award from the Real Estate Staging Association for her work and contributions to the industry

Currently six US colleges across the country endorse the program. Her book, *Home Staging for Dummies®*, has also been selected as the textbook on staging at several colleges in Canada.

Christine's success stems from her work ethic, desire for excellence, integrity and integral goodness. In a very competitive industry, what sets CSP apart are the differentiators and the driving force to be of service and value to the student. From the outset, CSP International core values, mission, "pay it forward" philosophy and their apprenticeship program have been the catalyst for the myriad of differentiators which set CSP apart.

Christine has worked with TV House Doctor Ann Maurice. Many of Christine's graduates have appeared on popular HGTV real estate shows. She was recently certified to facilitate Michael E Gerber's "Dreaming Room" event, was interviewed by Michael, and had a guest appearance on The Michael E Gerber Show. She also has appeared on ABC, NBC, CBS and FOX television affiliates.